GALATIANS

**A FIERY
RESPONSE TO
A STRUGGLING
CHURCH**

CARL P. COSAERT

REVIEW AND HERALD® PUBLISHING ASSOCIATION

Since 1861 | www.reviewandherald.com

Published by Review and Herald® Publishing Association, Hagerstown, MD 21741-1119

Review and Herald® titles may be purchased in bulk for educational, business, fund-raising, or sales promotional use. For information, e-mail SpecialMarkets@reviewandherald.com.

The Review and Herald® Publishing Association publishes biblically based materials for spiritual, physical, and mental growth and Christian discipleship.

The author assumes full responsibility for the accuracy of all facts and quotations as cited in this book.

This book was
Edited by Gerald Wheeler
Copyedited by James Cavil
Designed by Warren Rood
Cover art by Lars Justinen, www.goodsalt.com
Typeset: Bembo 11/13

PRINTED IN U.S.A.
15 14 13 12 11   5 4 3 2 1

Scripture quotations in this book, unless otherwise indicated, are from *The Holy Bible,* English Standard Version, copyright © 2001 by Crossway Bibles, a division of Good News Publishers. Used by permission. All rights reserved.

Scripture quotations marked NASB are from the *New American Standard Bible,* copyright © 1960, 1962, 1963, 1968, 1971, 1972, 1973, 1975, 1977, 1995 by The Lockman Foundation. Used by permission.

Texts credited to NIV are from the *Holy Bible, New International Version.* Copyright © 1973, 1978, 1984, International Bible Society. Used by permission of Zondervan Bible Publishers.

Texts credited to NKJV are from the New King James Version. Copyright © 1979. 1980, 1982 by Thomas Nelson, Inc. Used by permission. All rights reserved.

Scripture quotations marked NLT are taken from the *Holy Bible,* New Living Translation, copyright © 1996, 2004. Used by permission of Tyndale House Publishers, Inc., Carol Stream, Illinois 60188. All rights reserved.

Bible texts credited to NRSV are from the New Revised Standard Version of the Bible, copyright © 1989 by the Division of Christian Education of the National Council of the Churches of Christ in the U.S.A. Used by permission.

Bible texts credited to Phillips are from J. B. Phillips: *The New Testament in Modern English,* Revised Edition. © J. B. Phillips 1958, 1960, 1972. Used by permission of Macmillan Publishing Co., Inc.

Bible texts credited to RSV are from the Revised Standard Version of the Bible, copyright © 1946, 1952, 1971, by the Division of Christian Education of the National Council of the Churches of Christ in the U.S.A. Used by permission.

Library of Congress Cataloging-in-Publication Data
Cosaert, Carl P., 1968-   .
   Galatians : a fiery response to a struggling church / Carl P. Cosaert.
      p. cm.
   Includes bibliographical references and index.
   1. Bible. N.T. Galatians—Criticism, interpretation, etc. I. Title.
   BS2685.52.C67 2011
   227'.406—dc22
                                2010034126

ISBN 978-0-8280-2560-7

To Carol

My loving wife and best friend

PROVERBS 31:8–31

CONTENTS

CHAPTER 1

Saul of Tarsus—
From Christian
Persecutor to Apostle

Saul of Tarsus, aka the apostle Paul, was without a doubt the single most influential person in the life of the early church (outside of Jesus, of course).[1] The church first felt Saul's impact as a persecutor of the followers of Jesus, bringing hatred, imprisonment, stoning, and even death, and then as a follower of Jesus Himself, proclaiming the good news of God's grace and love. The change in Saul's life was so sudden and radical that many Christians were suspicious, wondering if the transformation was genuine, or some sort of Machiavellian ploy designed to work even greater havoc on the church. The change, however, was genuine, so much so that God used His new disciple to spread the news of Jesus to both Jews and Gentiles all across the Mediterranean world, as well as inspiring him to write at least 13 letters that today make up almost half of the books in the New Testament.

In this book we get to examine one of the most beloved and well-known letters written by Paul, one that may in fact be the first epistle he wrote—his letter to the Christians in Galatia. But before we begin looking at it, we need to spend a little time considering the man behind the letter. Just who was this Paul, or Saul of Tarsus? What do we know about his life before he decided to follow Jesus? Why was he so determined at one point to destroy the Christian faith? And what was it that suddenly compelled him radically to change course and decide to become a follower of Jesus?

We have two key sources of information on Paul's life: his extant letters and the stories about him found in the book of Acts. While Christians have long valued both sources, some scholars question whether we can accept the description of the apostle Paul in the book of Acts as trustworthy.

Therefore, before examining what we can know about the apostle's life, we must first consider why we can trust Luke's description in Acts as a reliable account of Paul. After that, we will see what we can learn about Paul's early years and discover what prompted him to persecute the

Christians so zealously. Finally, we shall turn our attention to the event that changed him forever.

The Reliability of Acts as a Source for Understanding Paul

In addition to the details we can gather about Paul from his own letters, we can also confidently rely on the book of Acts as a trustworthy source of information on his life for the following reasons.

1. *Luke's Stated Purpose.* The book of Acts is the second of a two-part work that begins by tracing the ministry of Jesus in the Gospel of Luke, and then recounts the growth and development of the early church in Acts. The first five verses at the beginning of Luke's Gospel serve as a prologue to both Luke and Acts. In it Luke describes the careful and thorough research he did before authoring his own account. Notice what he tells us: "Inasmuch as many have undertaken to compile a narrative of the things that have been accomplished among us, just as those who from the beginning were eyewitnesses and ministers of the word have delivered them to us, it seemed good to me also, having followed all things closely for some time past, to write an orderly account for you, most excellent Theophilus" (Luke 1:1-3). Here we learn that Luke not only interviewed eyewitnesses, but that he examined other written accounts, and that he closely (the Greek word means "accurately") reported all these events with the purpose of giving a reliable account.

While we do not have access to any of the sources Luke used in writing Acts, we can test his level of accuracy by examining one of the sources he consulted in writing his Gospel—the Gospel of Mark. A careful examination of the stories shared by Mark and Luke reveal not merely two separate accounts, but Luke's literary dependence on Mark. And wherever Luke relies on Mark, it is abundantly clear that Luke was a careful writer who strove to faithfully reproduce his sources without fundamentally distorting or altering them (compare, for example, Mark 5:21-42 and Luke 8:40-56, or Mark 9:38-41 and Luke 9:49, 50). It is certainly reasonable to assume that Luke maintained the same level of accuracy with his sources for Acts.[2]

2. *Luke Was an Eyewitness.* While Luke had to consult eyewitnesses for much of his information in the Gospel of Luke, he appears to have been a participant in many of the events associated with Paul in Acts, and he even was a follower of Paul himself. Evidence that Luke was an eyewitness appears in the "we passages" in Acts—those places where the pronoun switches from the third person "he" or "they" to the first person "we" (Acts 16:10-17; 20:5-15; 21:1-18; 27:1-28:16). The use of "we" in such passages suggests that at these specific points in Paul's missionary travels

Luke personally accompanied the apostle. Thus Luke not only knew Paul personally, but would have been acquainted with the apostle's other traveling companions. Luke's familiarity with Paul and his associates certainly provided him with an abundance of trustworthy information.

3. *Luke's Reliability in Historical Detail.* In an age when access to libraries and works of reference was virtually nonexistent, a careless writer would have had numerous opportunities to unintentionally fill his narrative with all kinds of historical blunders and anachronisms, such as those found in the fictional Gospel of Thomas or the Gospel of Peter, written in the second century. Instead, modern historians have confirmed that the book of Acts reveals an amazingly accurate use of small historical detail. For example, during his description of Paul's travels, Luke correctly identifies Cyprus, Achaia, and Asia as senatorial and not imperial provinces (Acts 13:4-7; 18:12; 19:31-38). He goes on to accurately describe Philippi as a Roman colony (Acts 16:12), the leaders of Thessalonica as "politarchs" (a term skeptics once proclaimed as a historical blunder, but now verified as true by the discovery of several inscriptions, see Acts 17:6, 8), the leaders in Ephesus rightly identified as Asiarchs (Acts 19:31), while Luke correctly designates the chief official on Malta as the "chief man" (Acts 28:7). The accuracy in this type of detail also encompasses the more general descriptions and terminology associated with early Christianity during the first century A.D. (e.g., Acts 2:36; 3:20; 4:27 refer to Jesus as the "Messiah" and the church as "the Way" in Acts 9:2; 19:9, 23; 24:14, 22). The reliability of such details gives us confidence that Luke's account as a whole is trustworthy.

4. *So-called Discrepancies Between Acts and Paul's Letters Have Been Overemphasized.* The primary difficulty that leads some scholars to question Luke's reliability as a firsthand witness boils down to what they believe are fundamental discrepancies between the Paul of Acts and the picture that the apostle provides of himself in his letters. They include the following: (1) Paul is clearly a letter writer, yet Acts never describes him in that way, and Luke never appears to make use of the apostle's letters as a source for his account; (2) Paul never explicitly mentions in his letters his missionary strategy of proclaiming the gospel in Jewish synagogues first and then focusing his attention on Gentiles; (3) Paul's Roman citizenship plays a fundamental role in his missionary travels in Acts, but he never alludes to it even once in his letters; and the fact that (4) Paul's concerns in Acts seem to differ from those in his letters.

While we clearly find differences between the material in Acts and that in Paul's letters, they are not as significant as some claim. First, one needs to realize that Luke is clearly selective in the material he shares—he had to be. As it is, Luke covers nearly four years in the opening chapters, and the entire book spans about 30 years—and that span of time does not even include the events that ultimately led to Paul's death. Obviously Luke knew more than he was able to share. We should not interpret his silence as a lack of knowledge that somehow makes his account untrustworthy.

In addition, any contrasts between Paul's concerns in Acts and those in his letters should really not surprise us, since the apostle is largely speaking to two different audiences. The book of Acts typically describes Paul as speaking to non-Christians while he wrote his letters specifically to Christians. And in those places in Acts where Paul does address a community of Christians (such as his speech to the Christian leaders from Ephesus recorded in Acts 20) a strong similarity with the concerns developed in his letters is apparent.

And why did Luke apparently not rely on Paul's letters as a source for his book? No one knows for sure, but there might have been a number of possible reasons. Luke may not have found the letters that significant for his historical narrative, and he may have felt they were too personal to use anyway. It is also a possibility that while Luke was still writing his account the letters were not easily accessible, since they had not yet had widespread circulation. Whatever the case may be, it does not invalidate what Luke does tell us.

While I do not believe such so-called discrepancies undermine the trustworthiness of Acts description of Paul, it does not mean that we can presently align everything in Acts with Paul's letters. One of the greatest difficulties occurs when trying to come up with a chronology of his travels based on what we find in Acts and what Paul tells us in his letters. While we can reconstruct a general outline of his life and ministry, we simply do not have all the pieces of the puzzle, a fact that makes those that we do have all the more valuable. We certainly have more than enough evidence to accept Luke's account as accurate and trustworthy.

Paul's Early Years

Saul (his original name) was born into the home of a devoutly religious Jewish family and spent the earliest years of his life growing up in Tarsus, the capital city of the Roman province of Cilicia (Acts 21:39). Tarsus was a Greek town well known in his day for its interest in education and philosophy. Although living several hundred miles away from the borders of the Holy Land, Saul's parents, descendants of the tribe of Benjamin, carefully avoided assimilating into the local culture. They followed the instructions given to Abraham and circumcised their son when he was eight days old (Phil. 3:5), and made sure that although he learned Greek, his first language was their native tongue (Acts 26:14). Although we commonly refer to him as Paul, his Jewish birth name was Saul, which may suggest that his parents named him after his legendary tribal ancestor, the first king of Israel. References in Acts 7:58 and Philemon 9 suggest that he was probably born around A.D. 5.

Unlike Jesus, however, Saul was not from a home of limited means. On the contrary, indications suggest that his family not only had some degree of wealth, but that they were well respected in their community. Citizenship in the ancient world was an honor granted to few provincials, yet Saul states that he was not only a citizen of Tarsus, but even more important, he had been born a Roman citizen. Roman citizenship was greatly desired since it guaranteed special prerogatives that few possessed: the right to vote, to own property, to have a fair and public trial, and a host of other legal privileges. While citizenship could be earned or given for a variety of reasons, custom still required that the individual granted citizenship have at least enough means to own property valued at 500 drachmas, an amount equal to approximately a day laborer's income for two years.[3] Since Saul was born a citizen, he likely inherited this right from either his father and/or his grandfather, and would have had the benefit of it as he grew up.

Incidentally, Roman custom required that his parents officially register him as a Roman citizen nine days after his birth, which, in his case, means the day after he was circumcised. At the time of his registration, Saul would have received an official three-part Latin name. The only part of that name now known to us is Paul, which in Latin is *Paulus*. Therefore, depending on whom he was around, he would have been used to being called either Saul or Paul.

Saul's earliest religious training occurred at home and included the memorization of the Hebrew scriptures. When he turned 6 or 7 years old he would have learned to read and write at the local synagogue, where the Hebrew scriptures would have been his only schoolbook. At the age of 12 or 13 he would have received his bar mitzvah, the special rite that designated him as a son of the commandment. And around this same time he would have been formally introduced to the traditions of the fathers, a large collection of oral rules that stipulated how one should observe the law in the varied circumstance of life.[4]

At some point in time, Saul's religious training grew more formal when he decided to become a Pharisee and traveled to Jerusalem to study with Gamaliel, one of the prominent Pharisee leaders of his day (Acts 22:3;

Gal. 1:14). The Pharisees were a group of Jews who emphasized strict adherence to the Torah (Jewish law), especially as interpreted by the traditions of their ancestors. While some Pharisees were more lenient, Paul appears to have gravitated to the more militant group, one determined that it could help fulfill God's great prophecies to Israel by purifying Israel from all forms of disloyalty to His law.

Persecutor of Christians

While Saul was almost certainly studying in Jerusalem by the time of Jesus' crucifixion, it is impossible to know if he ever encountered His ministry firsthand. What is clear, however, is that after Jesus' death Saul became convinced that Christians were part of the fundamental problem that plagued Judaism. Things were not right in Israel. God had made many wonderful promises to His people about His coming kingdom (Dan. 2; Zech. 8:23; Isa. 40-55), but they remained unfulfilled. Although the Lord had liberated Israel from its Babylonian captivity and brought them back to their own native land, they were still little more than captives to the Romans. Saul was convinced that if Israel would only be more faithful to God, then He would intervene and make His promises a reality. And as far as Saul was concerned, there existed no more brazen form of unfaithfulness and apostasy in Israel than that practiced by the followers of Jesus. They claimed not only that Jesus was the promised Messiah and the true center of the Jewish faith, but also that He was God incarnate—an ideal completely ridiculous to Saul since the Romans had crucified Jesus like a common criminal.

Like Phinehas, whose zeal saved Israel from idolatry in Numbers 25, Saul determined to do all in his power to rid Israel of the insidious teaching of those who worshipped Jesus. Although Saul's persecution of the early church begins rather inconspicuously, as he merely holds the coats of Stephen's executioners, it quickly intensifies in severity. In fact, several of the words that Luke employed to describe Saul's actions paint the picture of a wild ferocious beast, or a pillaging soldier bent on the destruction of his opponent. The word translated "ravaging" in Acts 8:3, for example, appears in the Greek translation of the Old Testament (Ps. 80:13) to describe the uncontrolled and destructive behavior of a wild boar. And the Jewish historian Josephus often uses the word translated "havoc" in Acts 9:21 and "destroy" in Galatians 1:13, 23 to depict those soldiers who show no restraint in their brutality against their opponents and their land.

Saul's crusade against the Christians was clearly not a halfhearted matter of convenience. He was more than willing to throw men, women, and

14

children into prison, and even to speak against them when they faced capital punishment (Acts 9:1, 2, 13, 14, 21; 22:4, 5; 26:9-11). His zeal against the Christians even led him to seek and to receive authorization from the chief priests to hunt down Christians who lived outside Judea. His actions make it clear that he sought to exterminate the Christian faith.

We can see a modern-day example of the mentality that prompted Saul to persecute early Christians so violently in the 1995 assassination of Israeli prime minister Yitzhak Rabin. In an attempt to bring an end to the hostilities between Jews and Palestinians and lasting peace, Rabin had decided to surrender portions of the land of Israel to Palestinian control. Rabin's murderer was a young man who, like Saul, was a student of the Torah, the Jewish law. Yigal Amir was convinced that in taking Rabin's life he was acting in the service of God as a true patriot of Israel. Amir viewed Rabin's decision to give away land that the Lord God had presented to their ancestors as an act of rebellion. And as Saul believed of the early Christians, Amir concluded that he must stop Rabin no matter what the cost.

Transformed by the Risen Christ

The possibility of Saul's conversion to Christianity would have been, from a human perspective, a most unlikely event—yet it happened! As he neared Damascus to persecute the Christians there, God changed his life forever.

The story of the future apostle's transformation is of such importance that Luke repeats it three separate times (Acts 9:1-19; 22:6-16; 26:12-18). It is important to note, however, that Saul's conversion did not occur out of nowhere, nor was it forced. Saul was no atheist. Rather he was a religious man, though gravely mistaken in his understanding of God. Jesus' words to him ("It is hard for you to kick against the goads" [Acts 26:14]) indicate that the Spirit had been already convicting Saul. In the ancient world a "goad" was a stick with a sharp point used to prod oxen whenever they resisted plowing. While Saul had fought against God's prodding for some time, finally on his way to Damascus, through a miraculous encounter with the risen Jesus, he chose to cease his struggle.

But what happened that transformed the entire course of his life? A careful study of the three accounts of his conversion indicates that he changed for two significant reasons.

First, although Saul had heard a lot about Jesus, and may have even witnessed Him during the final days leading up to His crucifixion, it was not until his trip to Damascus that Saul encountered the *risen* Christ for the first time. In fact, in his letters he is adamant that he did not merely see a vision, or simply hear a "voice." He actually witnessed the risen and glorified Lord with his own eyes (1 Cor. 15:8; Gal. 1:16). When this occurred, Saul suddenly realized that his whole life was completely upside down. The shocking fact that Jesus was really resurrected changed everything. It meant that He truly was the Messiah, and that His death on the cross was not a defeat but the glorious means by which God had overthrown the powers of sin and death—the real enemy that plagued His people. All the promises that Paul was trying to help God fulfill had already been established in Jesus, and in Jesus God's kingdom had already been inaugurated. Instead of helping God, Saul had been working against Him!

But something else also changed Saul. He not only encountered the risen Christ for himself—but he also experienced the "call" of Christ. The Greek word for "call" can mean a number of different things in the New Testament. It can refer to a person's name or nickname (Matt. 1:21; Luke 6:15), an invitation (Matt. 22:2-10; Luke 14:16-25), or even as part of the spiritual act of "calling" on God (Rom. 10:13). But in the nearly 50 times that Paul uses "call," he usually has in mind God's divine calling on a person's life (Gal. 1:13-15; Rom. 1:1, 7). And that is exactly what Saul experienced on the road to Damascus. He not only encountered the risen Jesus for himself, but also heard His call for his life (Acts 26:16-18; 22:10; 9:6). God had a plan for his life that gave him the peace that had been missing in his heart. It was his awareness and certainty of that call that gave him the strength and confidence he needed to stand up against all the opposition and hardship he would experience as a follower of Jesus.

The Gospel Goes to the Gentiles

Now to be known forever as Paul, he wasted no time in proclaiming the gospel. All the energy that he poured into persecuting Christians he now redirected to spreading the good news of Jesus. After spending several years in Arabia and then back again in Damascus, Paul journeyed to Jerusalem to visit with the apostles. Unsure about the sincerity of his conversion, they encouraged him to return to his hometown in Tarsus. And so Paul did, for more than five years. It is hard to say what took place during that period. But based on his comments in Galatians 1:21, it appears that he was preaching the gospel in the regions of Syria and Cilicia. Some have suggested that it was during this time that his family perhaps disinherited him (cf. Phil. 3:8), and he suffered a number of the hardships he describes in 2 Corinthians 11:23-28. Whatever happened during those years in Tarsus, God was obviously preparing Paul for a far greater sphere of influence. Ironically enough, it would bring him face to face with some of the Christians who had fled from his persecution in Jerusalem.

The persecution that broke out in Jerusalem after Stephen's death caused a number of Jewish believers to flee 300 miles north to Antioch in Syria. With a cosmopolitan population of some 500,000 inhabitants, Antioch was an ideal location for a church. As the group of believers in Antioch increased during the next several years, something unusual began to take place. Gentiles became attracted to the gospel. Unsure about the situation, the apostles in Jerusalem sent Barnabas up to Antioch to assess the situation.

A Basic Chronology of Paul's Missionary Activities

Date	Event	Biblical Reference
A.D. 34	Paul's call	Acts 9.1-19, Gal. 1.15, 16
34-37	Paul in Damascus and Arabia	Acts 9:20-25; Gal. 1:17
37-43	Paul in Tarsus and Cilicia	Gal. 1:21
43-47	Paul in Antioch	Acts 11:26-13:3
47-48	Paul's first missionary journey	Acts 13:3-14:26
48	Paul writes Galatians (?)	Gal. 1:1, 2
49-51	Paul's second missionary journey	Acts 15:41-18:22
51-57	Paul's third missionary journey	Acts 18:23-21:8
57-59	Paul imprisoned in Caesarea	Acts 23:33-26:32
59-60	Paul's journey to Rome	Acts 27:1-28:16
60-62	Paul's first Roman imprisonment	Acts 28:14-31
62-64	Paul's later travels	
64-65	Paul's arrest and death in Rome	2 Tim. 4:16, 17

Shortly after arriving in Antioch, Barnabas recognized that the Spirit of God was indeed drawing Gentiles to the gospel. If such evangelism among the Gentiles was to reach its full potential, Barnabas needed to find

someone thoroughly acquainted with the Gentile world but also committed to Jesus. His thoughts immediately went to Paul, who was only a short
distance away in Tarsus.

Needless to say, Paul accepted the invitation. And as the saying goes,
the rest is history. His ministry in Antioch blossomed. The church not only
grew, but became the missionary base from which he would spread the
gospel to Gentiles living all across the Mediterranean. While constructing
a chronology of Paul's life has its difficulties, the chart above provides a
basic overview of his missionary activities and the probable dates for them.

Encountering the Risen Christ

Paul was changed on the Damascus road because it was there that he
encountered the risen Christ and clearly heard and accepted the divine call
for his life. Interestingly, those are the same two ingredients that must accompany the life of every follower of Jesus. I do not mean that every
Christian has to have a dramatic conversion story—certainly not. But the
Bible does teach that every believer must have a personal experience with
the risen Jesus. For some it may be spectacular; for others it might be like
the rising of the sun, a continuously growing appreciation of God's love.
Whatever the case, each of us must encounter the risen Christ for ourselves. We cannot rely on the experience of others. Like Paul, we too need
to hear His call. For some that call might be a quiet whisper, or a series of
circumstances through which God confronts us with the need for some
sort of change in our life. It might be a summons to follow Him for the
first time in baptism, or maybe rebaptism. For others the call may be to a
deeper and more meaningful experience with Jesus. Whatever the case,
God's call is not a one-time experience—it comes at various times in our
lives and always leads us closer to Him.

---

[1] I want to thank my colleagues Dave Thomas and Bruce Johanson at Walla Walla
University for the time they spent reading and making comments on this manuscript. I especially owe a debt of gratitude to my good friend Bob Strom, whose extensive feedback
and suggestions were invaluable.

[2] I have drawn this and the following information on the historical reliability of Acts from
the following sources: D. A. Carson et al., *An Introduction to the New Testament* (Grand
Rapids: Zondervan, 1992), pp. 181-213; Colin J. Hemer, *The Book of Acts in the Setting of
Hellenistic History* (Eisenbrauns, 1990); and John Drane, *Introducing the New Testament*
(Minneapolis: Fortress Press, 2001), pp. 257-264.

[3] John McRay, *Paul: His Life and Teaching* (Grand Rapids: Baker Academic, 2003), p. 24.

[4] *Ibid.*, pp. 34, 35.

CHAPTER 2

Paul's Authority and Gospel

While you certainly cannot judge a book by its cover, Nancy Pearl, a well-known librarian from Seattle, believes that its opening lines can usually give a pretty good indication if it is really worth the read. In an interview several years ago on National Public Radio's *Morning Edition*, she went as far as to claim, "I think when you read a good first line it's like falling in love with somebody. Your heart starts pounding . . . it opens up all the possibilities."[1]

Has a book ever grabbed you with its opening lines in such a way that it left a permanent impression on you? Certain books are well known for their memorable opening lines. For example, who would not recognize the beginning words of Charles Dickens' classic novel *The Tale of Two Cities:* "It was the best of times, it was the worst of times . . ." But while I have come across a number of intriguing opening lines, I can honestly say that no *novel* has ever moved me in the dramatic fashion that Nancy Pearl describes.

There is, however, one opening line that has overwhelmed me with all kinds of possibilities. And I am not the only one to have been mesmerized by it. It captivated the hearts of the earliest Christians and has continued to bring hope to countless others ever since it was first penned—the opening lines of the New Testament.

But before you instinctively begin to think about the Gospel of Matthew and the puzzling genealogy introducing it, let me direct your attention elsewhere. While Matthew is the first book of the present arrangement of the New Testament, it was not the first written. It is important to remember that the writings that comprise the New Testament are not in chronological order. The earliest New Testament writings are the letters of the apostle Paul, though the Epistle of James may also be quite early. The four Gospels probably did not appear until after Paul's death, around A.D. 65.

19

Thus the opening lines I am referring to are found in Paul's letter to the Galatians.

Some scholars differ as to whether Galatians or 1 Thessalonians is earlier. I am personally convinced that Paul penned Galatians around A.D. 48 after his first missionary journey and before the council in Jerusalem mentioned in Acts 15. An early date for Galatians corresponds easily with Paul's first missionary journey described in Acts, and it explains several statements he makes in Galatians about his visits to Jerusalem. But in regard to our interest in the opening lines of the New Testament, it really makes no difference because all of Paul's letters roughly begin in the same way. The chart below gives an approximate timeline for Paul's epistles.

A Basic Time Line of Paul's Letters

Second Missionary Journey	Third Missionary Journey	First Roman Imprisonment	Paul's Later Travels	Paul's Second Roman Imprisonment		
48?	50	55	57	60-62	62-64	65
Galatians	Thessalonians	Corinthians	Romans	The Prison Epistles	1 Timothy & 2 Timothy Titus	

In this chapter we will focus our attention on the spiritual significance found in Paul's initial greeting to the Galatians, and how it prepares us for what to expect in the rest of his letter. But before we do that, it is important that we first look at Paul as a letter writer.

Paul the Letter Writer

As we begin our study of Galatians, we need to recognize that Galatians is an actual letter. When Paul started writing, he was not trying to produce some literary masterpiece that later generations would admire as a classical piece of literature. Under the guidance of the Spirit, Paul was composing a real letter addressing specific situations that involved him and the believers in Galatia. Therefore, as we seek to understand the message that his epistle has for us today, it is vital that we first consider what it would have meant to the Christians in Galatia.

Letters such as the Epistle to the Galatians played an essential role in Paul's apostolic ministry. As the missionary to the Gentile world, he founded a number of churches scattered around the Mediterranean. Although he did his best to visit them whenever he could, it was simply impossible for him to be in any one place for too long. To compensate for his physical absence, Paul wrote letters to the various congregations in order to give them guidance and direction. They were of great value to the churches who received them, and believers quickly recognized them as being inspired Scripture (2 Peter 3:15, 16). As time passed, people shared copies of them with other congregations. While some of Paul's letters have vanished (cf. Col. 4:16), 13 survive in the New Testament.

At one time some Christians believed that the format of Paul's letters was unique—a special one created by the Holy Spirit in order to contain God's inspired Word. While this made sense to many, it all changed in 1897 when two young scholars from Oxford, Bernard Grenfell and Arthur Hunt, accidentally discovered in an out-of-the-way Egyptian town known as Oxyrhynchus some 500,000 fragments of ancient papyri, a popular writing material, dating back to several hundred years before and after Christ. In addition to some of the oldest copies of the New Testament writings, they also found ancient invoices, tax returns, receipts, and even personal letters. Surprisingly to some, the basic format of Paul's letters turned out to be the identical format used by all letter writers in his day. It included the following elements: (1) an opening salutation that mentioned the sender, the recipient, and then a greeting; (2) a word of thanksgiving; (3) the main body of the letter; and finally (4) a closing remark.

While Paul's letters follow the basic pattern of letters of his time, he injects a distinctly Christian perspective into them. And while they do what every other letter did, the way they did it was significant. With this in mind, let us now look at the opening lines of Galatians.

A Unique Greeting

As we consider the epistle's opening lines we need to bypass the first two verses because they do not really comprise what we would consider as the opening lines of the letter. As I already mentioned, in antiquity authors always began a letter by stating their own name followed by the name of the person or people being addressed. So verses 1 and 2 really function more like the title page of a modern book.

The opening line of the letter proper really begins in verse 3, in which Paul says, "Grace to you and peace from God our Father and the Lord

21

Jesus Christ, who gave himself for our sins to deliver us from the present evil age, according to the will of our God and Father, to whom be the glory forever and ever. Amen" (Gal. 1:3-5).

What makes this greeting so significant? Sure, they may be the first words of the New Testament, but are they really that noteworthy? Is not Paul just making use of a typical friendly greeting, something akin to the way many people often begin a letter today by saying, "Dear So-and-So"? Everyone knows that is just a standard introduction. Very few would really think that the word "dear" at the beginning of a modern letter was really a term of genuine affection. It is just a formality.

Paul's greeting, however, is no mere formality. When he says, "Grace to you and peace from God our Father and the Lord Jesus Christ," he is not using a standard, generic greeting. That is what makes the apostle's statement so surprising. In all the documents and letters that have survived down through the centuries, this greeting occurs first in Paul's writings. Other Jewish letters, for example, offer greetings of health and peace, but we never find this combination of grace and peace before Paul. And what is more, his use of grace and peace in Galatians is not just an accidental, one-time occurrence. He uses the exact same phrase at the beginning of each of the letters attributed to him.

What is even more interesting is that his greeting appears to be a deliberate play on words.

Typically ancient letters would begin with the initial word "greetings." Acts 23:26 and James 1:1 offer examples. In Greek the English word translated as "greetings" is *chairein*. Paul, however, replaces the typical word for greeting that his readers would have expected and replaces it with a similar sounding word—but one with vastly different connotations. Instead of *chairein*, Paul writes "*charis*," translated as, "grace."

To this he then adds the typical Jewish greeting, "peace." We see an example of the typical Hebrew greeting in 1 Samuel 25:5: "So David sent ten young men. And David said to the young men, 'Go up to Carmel, and go to Nabal and greet him in my name. And thus you shall greet him: "Peace be to you, and peace be to your house, and peace be to all that you have."'"

But for Paul it is not just grace and peace, but grace and peace to you from God the Father and the Lord Jesus Christ.

So we have established that the apostle's greeting is unique. But what does it mean? What is grace? And what does the word "peace" imply?

Grace

"Grace" is one of Paul's favorite words. He uses it more than any other New Testament writer. Of the more than 150 times the word occurs in the New Testament, about 100 of them appear in his letters. While words like "justification" and the "cross" are certainly important terms for Paul, they are not present in all of his letters. The word "cross" occurs only 10 times in Paul's epistles, and not once in 2 Corinthians, 1 or 2 Thessalonians, 1 or 2 Timothy, or even Titus. He uses "justification" sparingly as well. But the situation is different with the word "grace." It appears in every one of his 13 letters. No matter how different the problems he faces in each letter, grace is so central to his gospel message that it is always part of his response.

But what is this grace that Paul talks so frequently about? Unfortunately, he never gives a precise definition of it. So where can we go to get a solid picture of grace? Seeing how Jesus uses a word can often be helpful, but not in this case. Although John 1:14 says Jesus' life was the epitome of grace, the word "grace" does not occur even once in the words of Jesus recorded in the Gospels.

If we want to understand the full dimension of what grace involves for Paul, we have to go back to the Old Testament. Remember that Paul was a Jew who had studied to be a rabbi. He was well versed in the Hebrew Scriptures, and it is there that we find a concrete picture of what grace is all about.

The word "grace" appears to have originated in connection with the old Hebrew verb *hānā*, which literally means "to bend down or to stoop." It conveys the idea of someone bending down to help someone who has fallen, or is in need—and typically that of a superior to an inferior. Eventually this verbal concept of bending down became a noun meaning "favor" or "grace." But not just any kind of favor—rather, a heartfelt response of unconditional love and caring bestowed upon someone unable to help themselves. And here is what is so amazing—in the Old Testament it is God who is typically described as the one who extends the favor or grace (Gen. 6:8; 39:21; Ex. 33:12; Ps. 51:1). I like the way the late bible scholar Donald Barnhouse is credited with explaining it: "Love that goes upward is worship; love that goes outward is affection; but love that stoops is grace."[2]

What is grace then for Paul? It is the act of extending favor or kindness to one who does not deserve it and who could never earn it. Grace is not treating someone as he or she deserves, but showing kindness, favor, and forgiveness to those who do not deserve it. Ultimately for Paul it is the un-merited favor of God, who bends down to forgive us our sins and freely gives us His own righteousness.

Peace

What about the word "peace"? When Paul speaks about peace, he is not referring to a cessation of activity or stillness, such as we might envision when we talk about water being peaceful, or the peace before a storm. No, when Paul talks about peace he is once again drawing upon his knowledge of the Hebrew Scriptures. The Hebrew word usually translated by the English word peace is "šālôm." In fact, the Hebrew word has been directly transliterated in the English language as "shalom." As mentioned earlier, this was the typical Hebrew greeting. People would meet each other with the word "shalom."

But shalom is far richer than our modern greeting of "hi" or "hello." Shalom, and its family of related words, are some of the most theologically important ones used in the Old Testament. In fact, its meaning is so rich that it is impossible to convey all that it means in a single English word. It is not merely the absence of war—it points to the positive sense of unhin-dered unity and harmony. Such peace means to be complete, to be whole, to be full, to prosper, to be in health, to be in harmony, to be well in the fullest sense of the term.

Two Chronicles 25:2 provides a good illustration of the meaning of "shalom." The passage describes an assessment of the reign of king Amaziah, the son of king Joash. Notice how it describes him: "And he did what was right in the eyes of the Lord, yet not with a *whole* heart." The Hebrew literally declares that Amaziah did what was right in the Lord's sight but not with a "šālēm" heart. Here we see that the word "šālēm" (closely related to "shalom") means a whole, or undivided, heart.

How does one acquire this kind of peace, this wholeness? The Hebrew Scriptures are clear. True peace has its source only in God. He is the one who speaks peace to His people (Ps. 85:8). Not something that we can achieve ourselves, it only comes as a gift that He alone gives (1 Chron. 22:9, 10; Num. 6:24-26).

A Divine Order

Grace and peace. We cannot put these two words in any other sequence. It is a divine order. First grace and then peace. It can happen in no other way. Unless God first showers us with His grace, forgiving us our sins and

24

covering our sinful lives with the perfect life of His son, we can have no true peace. Our peace, our wholeness, is rooted in His grace, and His grace alone.

I cannot think of a more powerful way to begin the New Testament! In just two simple words, Paul encapsulates the entire essence of what the message of the cross is all about. God offers grace and peace to every descendant of Adam and Eve. He is not at war with the human race (Rom. 5:1)—He is not against us. God bears no grudges. Rather, He has already accomplished everything necessary for the salvation of the human race in His Son, Jesus, the divine Son of God, who stooped down from heaven to take our fallen humanity upon Himself, and who even stooped down to be nailed upon a cross that by His death we might be able to hear those much-needed words spoken to us: "Grace to you and peace from God the Father and our Lord Jesus Christ."

A Preview of What's to Come

The opening salutation of Galatians also prepares us for the key themes that Paul will develop throughout the rest of the letter, as well as the particular challenge he faced in Galatia.

As we will see, certain troublemakers in Galatia challenged his authority and his gospel. These false teachers were not pleased with his message that salvation was based on faith in Christ alone. They felt that his teaching was undermining obedience to the law. But his opponents were subtle. Knowing that the foundation of Paul's gospel message was directly tied to the source of his apostolic authority, they determined to launch a powerful attack against it. Since the church in Antioch on the Orontes had been the one to send out Paul and Barnabas as missionaries (Acts 13:1-3), the false teachers in Galatia claimed that he was simply a messenger from Antioch—nothing more! Consequently, they argued, his message was merely his own opinion, not the Word of God.

Paul masterfully combats both challenges right in the midst of his opening salutation. Recognizing the potential danger such allegations posed if left unopposed, he expands his traditional salutation (longer than in any of his other letters) by stating that his apostleship originates neither with any ecclesiastical body nor with any single person. It resides in "Jesus Christ and God the Father" (Gal. 1:1).

But he does not stop there. Instead of merely commencing the letter with his customary greeting of "grace and peace," Paul also expands his greeting (once again, unlike any of his other letters) to state clearly what the gospel of grace and peace is all about. The grace and peace we have with God is not the result of our conformity to the law. Its sole basis rests on what Christ accomplished through His death and resurrection. They did something we could never do for ourselves. It broke the power of sin and death, freeing us from the evil of this age that holds so many in fear and bondage (verse 4).

For Paul the situation in Galatia was no laughing matter. In fact, he was so white-hot with passionate concern over the false picture of God that the false teachers were giving to the Galatians that he even skips the typical word of thanksgiving that is a part of all of his other salutations.

A Book Worth Reading

According to librarian Nancy Pearl, if a book is worth reading it must captivate you with its opening lines. It must make your heart begin to beat faster and open up all kinds of possibilities. What better example than what we find in the opening lines of Galatians? It invites us to experience for ourselves the full riches of the gift of grace and peace that God offers to us. And we don't have to wait until eternity to enjoy it—it is ours today.

---

[1] Nancy Pearl, "Famous First Words," National Public Radio's *Morning Edition,* Sept. 8, 2004.

[2] As quoted in Charles R. Swindoll, *The Grace Awakening* (Nashville: Word Publishing, 1990), p. 8.

CHAPTER 3

The Issue of Circumcision

The beginning of a new school year is always filled with a mixture of excitement and impatient anticipation as students eagerly wonder what it holds in store. This was certainly the case in 2007 as students began arriving at the Kiriani public high school, located just outside of Meru town in eastern Kenya. It all seemed promising at first as students helped each other move into their dorm rooms, making new friends and renewing old friendships along the way.

The signs of a promising year quickly disappeared, however, when an early-morning shower innocently revealed that one of the new boys was uncircumcised. In some cultures a discovery of this nature among a group of teenage boys would result only in some crude comments or a bunch of juvenile jokes, and that would be the end of it. But that was not the case in Kenya. It was no joking matter. The positive and friendly atmosphere that had begun the school year gave way to hostility as the other boys in the shower began chanting songs about war and circumcision. Fearing for his life, the terrified student, and eventually 17 other uncircumcised students, fled to the principal's office, where they ended up spending the night. The principal moved quickly to resolve the crisis—by expelling the uncircumcised students.

Although the principal's decision might surprise us, it illustrates the important role that circumcision plays in many cultures around the world today. In places such as Kenya it is far more than a matter of personal hygiene—it is a rite of passage marking a transition in social status from adolescence to adulthood. We can see the relationship between circumcision and a male's societal position in the letter the principal sent to the parents of the dismissed boys. "Just as you cannot keep your elder son who is circumcised with your young son who is not," the principal explained, "this also applies in the dormitory."[1]

Even though some government officials decried such "primitive" behavior in a public school, the majority of the local inhabitants agreed that uncircumcised boys should not participate in the same activities as those who have been circumcised. As one local tribal elder said: "They cannot bathe together, share towels, and on some occasions sit together to discuss issues."[2] In this kind of environment, circumcision is of utmost importance because it serves as a badge of identity, clearly defining a person's place in society—regardless of whether one agrees with the practice or not!

Although such strong opinions over circumcision seem rather odd, if not down right crazy, to most people in the Western world (I cannot, for example, imagine anyone in our culture ever advocating the expulsion of uncircumcised boys from school), it gives us a little sense of how emotionally charged and potentially hostile the situation was with the churches in Galatia.

Circumcision is the fundamental issue that Paul confronts in his letter to the Galatians. The situation in Galatia even shares some uncanny parallels with the story from Kenya. In both situations a more established group strongly believed that all newcomers should submit to the rite of circumcision, just as they themselves had done. The only real difference was the participants: in Kenya it was upperclassmen versus underclassmen, while in Galatia it was Jewish Christians versus new Gentile believers. And in the same way that the new students in Kenya were not welcome at the school unless they were first circumcised, so Gentiles were also not welcome and considered as genuine Christians and full-fledged members of the church family unless they were circumcised. In each case, circumcision had become a badge of identity—those who had it were "in," and those who did not were "out."

Beyond the basic similarities between the two accounts, the issue of circumcision and the events that Paul describes in Galatians 2:1-14 raises some important questions for us to consider in this chapter. First, why was circumcision, of all the possible issues, so important to a number of early Christians? And why did Paul strongly oppose having Gentile believers submit to it—even if they were willing? Did the issue really merit being a subject of discussion at a meeting between him and the leading apostles in Jerusalem? In addition, why would he publicly rebuke Peter over his decision to eat with fellow Jewish Christians who had just arrived from Jerusalem, instead of sharing a meal with uncircumcised Gentile believers? And finally, what is probably the most important question of all, why should believers living in the twenty-first century even care about a church

28

scuffle that happened nearly 2,000 years ago over an ancient custom such as circumcision?

The Origin of Circumcision in Judaism

While circumcision is of utmost importance in countries such as Kenya, it was (and is) of even greater importance in Judaism. Why? Although the origin of circumcision as an ancient ancestral custom in Kenya is shrouded in mystery, in Judaism the practice dates back not only to the ancestor of the Jewish race, but to a specific command given by God. Genesis 17 records the incident.

Circumcision was to be a sign of the everlasting covenant that God had made with Abraham and all his descendants. And the divine instructions about circumcision were quite specific. "Every male throughout your generations, whether born in your house or bought with your money from any foreigner who is not of your offspring, both he who is born in your house and he who is bought with your money, shall surely be circumcised" (Gen. 17:12, 13). The consequences for noncompliance were also severe: "Any uncircumcised male who is not circumcised in the flesh of his foreskin shall be cut off [a type of spiritual excommunication] from his people; he has broken my covenant" (verse 14). For this reason circumcision plays an even more fundamental role in Judaism than it does today in places such as Kenya. For Jews it certainly is not an issue of hygiene, or even a rite of passage. Rather, it is a direct command given by God and a sign of the covenant that He made with their forefather, Abraham, and all his descendants.

Why Was Paul So Upset?

Although understanding the divine origin of circumcision in Judaism reveals why Jews would feel strongly about it, it does not explain why Paul would speak so negatively about it in Galatians. Remember, Paul was Jewish himself—and he was not ashamed of it. In fact, he can speak highly of his Jewish upbringing and even of circumcision (Rom. 3:1, 2; 9:3-5; Phil. 3:4-6). So what would make Paul so upset with the circumstances in Galatia that he would exclaim, "Look: I, Paul, say to you that if you accept circumcision, Christ will be of *no advantage* to you" (Gal. 5:2)? In fact, Paul was so consumed with white-hot anger against those who insisted that Gentile believers submit to the knife of circumcision that he made an astonishing declaration: "I wish those who unsettle you would emasculate themselves!" (verse 12). When is the last time you heard your pastor say something like that to the entire congregation?

Simply put, Paul did not oppose circumcision as a divine institute given to the Jews—how could he, since it was, after all, God-given? In Acts 16:1-4, right after the council in Jerusalem declared that circumcision was not required of Gentiles, Paul even had Timothy, whose mother was Jewish, circumcised. Circumcision was not merely a good-versus-bad issue for him.

What infuriated Paul was the distorted position that ancient Judaism had bestowed upon circumcision. Approximately 170 years before Jesus' birth, during a time of severe persecution, the rite had become a prized symbol of national and religious identity. Palestine had fallen under the jurisdiction of Antiochus IV Epiphanes, a Greek ruler of ancient Syria. Antiochus had great plans for his kingdom, and exalted opinions about himself—some of his coins, for example, carried the inscription "Antiochus Theos Epiphanes" ("Antiochus who is god manifested"). In an attempt to unite his kingdom more closely together, he decreed that all his subjects should adopt the religious practices of the Greeks. As you can expect, many Jews refused to surrender their ancestral faith.

Antiochus issued another decree intended to stomp out the faith of the Jews. He forbade, under the penalty of death, the practice of the most distinguishing external aspects of the Jewish faith: circumcision, Sabbath, food laws, and the cultic services at the Temple. While many Jews were willing to compromise, others rose up in defense of their ancestral customs. The latter not only took up the sword against Antiochus—they also turned it against any fellow Jews willing to compromise. And of all the ancient laws, circumcision became the defining criterion of whether a person was a faithful son of Abraham.

Why circumcision and not something such as the Sabbath? Because of all the Old Testament laws, circumcision was, so to speak, the most black and white. Either a man was circumcised or he wasn't. It was simple and straightforward. Criteria such as the Sabbath, for example, were harder to pin down in actual practice. Circumcision was obvious.[3] It became another Shibboleth (see Judges 12:6), a defining indicator of a person's Jewish identity.

And it continued to be a badge of identity long after the Jews defeated their Syrian rulers, gained their own independence, and eventually came under the rule of the Roman Empire. During the brief years of their independence, zealous Jews not only forced all uncircumcised Jews in Palestine to be circumcised, but also required it of every man—whether he was Jewish or not—living in regions under Jewish jurisdiction. You can be sure that that did not leave many men with a positive view of Judaism! While God required circumcision of Abraham's literal descendants in the Old Testament, He never required it of Gentiles.

Some Jews even came to regard the mere act of circumcision as an automatic passport to salvation. A Jewish epigram from Jesus' day confidently claimed, "Circumcised men do not descend into Gehenna."[4]

With this historical context in mind, we can better understand why Paul so opposed the "forced practice" of circumcision in Galatia. The issue was not really circumcision in and of itself, but the question of identity. What should be the defining characteristic of a Christian? What role should circumcision have in the life of the Christian church?

The Defining Mark of the Christian

Identity was certainly not a pressing issue in the earliest days of the church. All of the followers of Jesus were Jews. And although ancient Judaism was certainly not monolithic in all its beliefs (consider, for example, the different views of Jewish groups such as the Pharisees, Sadducees, and the Essenes), all Jews were essentially united in their belief in the one Creator God, who had called Israel to be His special people and given them His laws. But when Gentiles began responding to the good news of Jesus, the issue of identity suddenly became an important one.

How "Jewish" did a Gentile have to become in order to be a "genuine" Christian? Was faith in Jesus alone sufficient, or did Gentiles also have to do something else—namely, submit to the Jewish law, which primarily boiled down in Paul's day to circumcision? What was to be the defining characteristic of the Christian faith?

Paul was convinced that the question had only one answer. The distinguishing mark that identifies whether someone is a Christian is not behavior—not what a person does or does not do (whether that be circumcision, or anything else, for that matter). A Christian will certainly do many good things, but according to Paul what ultimately makes one a Christian is not outward circumcision or any other behavior, but an inner circumcision of the heart (Deut. 30:6; Rom. 2:29), a living and vibrant faith in Jesus Christ.

With this in mind, let's briefly examine the events that Paul describes in Galatians 2:1-16.

Standing Firm for the Gospel

Confrontation is never easy. It makes little difference whether you are

31

giving it or receiving it. In fact, most people find it so uncomfortable that they choose to avoid it at all cost—sometimes even when it may be desperately needed. We have no reason to believe that Paul was any different in this regard. Sure, he was an apostle, and we have clear examples in his letters in which he really lets someone have it. Within the first two chapters of Galatians alone, for example, we find Paul flinging anathemas at the Galatians (Gal. 1:8, 9) and giving the apostle Peter a good public tongue-lashing (Gal. 2:11-14). On the basis of such incidents we might be tempted to compare him to some kind of religious hothead who thrived on confrontation.

While Paul could certainly oppose someone if necessary, it was not something that he enjoyed doing—especially when it was fellow believers in Jesus. In 2 Corinthians, for example, we learn that he made a painful journey to Corinth in an attempt to deal with some of the difficult problems he had written to them about in his first letter. That visit appears not to have gone well—for everyone involved. The apostle returned to Ephesus disappointed and wrote the Corinthians a letter about the encounter (apparently never preserved, though some scholars believe part of it survives in 2 Corinthians 10-13). Paul's comments in 2 Corinthians 2:1-4 reveal how difficult it was for him to have to confront the Corinthians, even when they were clearly in the wrong. "For I made up my mind not to make another painful visit to you. For if I cause you pain, who is there to make me glad. . . . For I wrote to you out of much affliction and anguish of heart and with many tears, not to cause you pain but to let you know the abundant love that I have for you." Although no other correspondence exists between Paul and the Galatians, one can only imagine that his feelings were no different.

If he did not enjoy confronting fellow believers, why then did he speak with such candor to the Galatians and Peter? We find the answer in an incident sandwiched right between his rebuke of the Galatians and Peter. It relates a trip that Paul made to Jerusalem and the private meeting he had there with Peter, James, and John. The purpose of the session was not merely a social visit. The apostle was concerned that accusations against his ministry by some Jewish Christians were ultimately an attack against the unity of the apostles, and thus the entire early church itself. In spite of the attempts of some to disrupt the proceedings, they were a success. The apostles acknowledged that God had called Paul to reach the Gentiles, just as He had chosen Peter to preach to the Jews. And although they focused on different groups of people, the gospel they proclaimed was the same.

Divide and conquer has always been one of the devil's most successful strategies. He used it to weaken and destroy the nation of Israel during the reign of Rehoboam (1 Kings 12), and he was trying it again in Paul's day to extinguish the light of the gospel. Recognizing the schemes of Satan behind the accusations of the troublemakers in Galatia and in Peter's behavior in Antioch, Paul did all in his power to oppose it—no matter how uncomfortable it made him.

Why were the accusations against Paul's ministry such a threat to the unity of the church? If his gospel was faulty, the implication was that the Gentiles brought into the church through his ministry were also "faulty" and therefore, in a sense, spiritually illegitimate. If that were true, it could lead only to two possible outcomes: (1) the Gentiles would have to submit to circumcision and then rejoin the church—an action that would have implied that faith in Jesus was not sufficient; or (2) the entire Gentile church would either split off from the original church in Jerusalem, or be reduced to merely second-class Christians—something similar to racial segregation in the United States after the Civil War. Whatever the case, Christ would be divided. Writing to the Galatians before the council in Jerusalem had as yet dealt with the issue (Acts 15), Paul knew that either option would ultimately destroy the church.

Peter's actions in Antioch were serious. At first glance his behavior would seem insignificant—all he did was move from one table to another at mealtime. What is so wrong with that? The problem was not that he merely wanted to visit with some old friends just arrived from Jerusalem, but that he did not want the circumcised Jewish Christians from Jerusalem to see him enjoying table fellowship with uncircumcised Gentile Christians. Can you imagine what spiritual message his actions would have conveyed to the Gentile believers?

It reminds me of an incident that happened to me when I was 13. I was in the seventh grade at the time and had fallen hopelessly in love with a girl named Christi, who lived just a few houses down the street. We were in the same classroom at school, and I was sure that she liked me. Christi often invited me to her house to talk or play—and we always had a wonderful time together. She even allowed me to walk her back and forth from school—well, at least part way. Whenever we reached main street, Christi always found some excuse for why we could not continue the rest of the way to school together. Although she never told me why, it was not hard for me to figure it out. Christi did not want her friends to see her with "me." It left me so dejected and hurt that even though it happened more than 30 years ago I still remember it as if it were yesterday. I felt I was just not quite good enough for her!

The Gentiles would have felt far worse. Peter's actions in Galatians 2 sent a clear message to them—they were not good enough in the eyes of God! They were second-class Christians. In a public manner he loudly proclaimed that Gentiles did not measure up because they were not circumcised. Faith in Christ was not sufficient. Recognizing all this, Paul was determined that the truth of the gospel and the unity of the church would not be destroyed so easily. He challenged Peter on the spot for turning the good news of the gospel for all into an exclusive spiritual clique centered on a person's behavior, rather than on faith in Jesus Christ.

---

[1] Noel Mwakugu, "Circumcision Row Divides Kenya Town." BBC News. [cited Jan. 30, 2008]. Online: http://newsvote.bbc.co.uk/mpapps/pagetools/print/news.bbc.co.uk/2/hi/africa/6367807.stm.

[2] *Ibid.*

[3] Tom Wright, *Paul for Everyone: Galatians and Thessalonians* (Louisville, Ky.: Westminster John Knox, 2004), p. 15.

[4] In C.E.B. Cranfield, *A Critical and Exegetical Commentary on the Epistle to the Romans* (Edinburgh: T. & T. Clark, 1975), p. 172.

CHAPTER 4

Our New Identity in Christ

It has happened to me twice, and I will never forget it. Twice I have been mistaken for someone else—and not just by some stranger, but by people I thought knew me. The first time was in Toronto, Canada, during a ministerial presession preceding an international religious conference in 2000. The convention hall where the main meeting took place was humongous and densely packed with people from all around the world. After finding a seat toward the back, I began glancing around to see if I could spot anyone I knew. But as hard as I looked, I could not see a single person I recognized. It made me feel completely lost, like a tiny speck of sand on a vast ocean beach. Then right as the meeting ended, I finally saw a face I recognized. It was someone I had known while I was pastoring in Minnesota. Suddenly I came to life. As difficult as it was, I fought my way through the crowd to greet my friend. When he saw me, his face lighted up, and he gave me a big hug. Quickly we caught each other up on how our wives and children were doing. I had such a warm feeling inside of me. Then it happened. He called me Barry and asked how I enjoyed pastoring in Colorado. At first I assumed that I had misunderstood what he said. So I asked him to repeat himself. And sure enough, he called me Barry again. I could not believe it. He thought I was someone else! As much as I hated to break the news to him, I told him I was not Barry from Colorado, but Carl from Indiana.

The same thing happened about three years later at the Carolina camp meeting when a former professor I had kept contact with through the years completely mistook me for someone else. After I pointed out his mistake, I got the feeling that he was not nearly as interested in our conversation as he had been earlier. Needless to say, both experiences left me feeling a little shaken—as if I had somehow lost my own distinct identity.

Identity is important. It is what defines us in contrast to a world filled with billions of other people. Our identity is the totality of all that we are—it consists of all our experiences, dreams, hopes, and aspirations. And we spend our entire lives building, enhancing, maintaining, and protecting our identity. That is what makes any massive upheaval in our personal lives so difficult. Moving, getting a new job, memory loss, or being separated from family, friends, or country can be some of the most traumatic events in life, because they force us, in varying degrees, both to lose and to reformulate who we are.[1]

The issue of our identity and the challenges that often face it strikes at the heart of what Paul describes in Galatians 2:15-21. The situation that divides him and the troublemakers in Galatia is not trivial. It is not merely a matter of different ideas about how a person should dress, eat, or even behave. Nor does it merely involve differences between a more liberal and a more conservative interpretation of the Jewish Scriptures. No, the issue in Galatia is far more basic and foundational. Ultimately it is about identity— a Christian's identity. As Tom Wright puts it: "It is a matter of *who you are in the Messiah*."[2]

Although Paul's basic overall point in Galatians 2:15-21 is fairly straight-forward, the way he develops his point is actually one of the most complex and theologically dense passages in all of his epistles. Thus while the passage is full of wonderful insights, it is also easy to get lost in the details. So before we dive into the passage, it is important to drop anchor so we will not lose our place when we come back to the surface.

The anchor to keep us from losing our way in Paul's complex discussion is the conclusion to his argument in Galatians 2:19, 20. "I have been crucified with Christ. It is no longer I who live, but Christ who lives in me. And the life I now live in the flesh I live by faith in the Son of God, who loved me and gave himself for me." Here the apostle declares that the Christian life is all about losing our old identity and embracing the new one that belongs to us in Christ. Or to put it another way, the Christian life is not essentially about what we do, but who we are *in Christ*. No matter how difficult or confusing Paul's comments in Galatians 2:15-21 may appear to be, it is important to remember that everything he says seeks to make this one main point. So with his conclusion as our anchor, let's look at the passage more closely.

A Rather Strange Beginning

At first glance his words seem rather strange. "We ourselves are Jews by birth and not Gentile sinners" (verse 15). How could Paul, the great advocate of equality in Christ (Gal. 3:28), actually state such a thing? It sounds completely out of character for him. How can he claim, in verse 20, that we all have a new identity in Christ, but seem to declare exactly the opposite in verse 14? Certainly the Jews are also sinners. In fact, the words in verse 14 sound like something that Peter or the visiting Jews from Jerusalem would have said—the "us" versus "them" theology that Paul just condemned in the behavior of Peter and Barnabas. What are we to make of it?

Paul's words make better sense if we look at them in their immediate context. In the previous verses he has just pointed out the error of Peter and Barnabas' behavior in treating the uncircumcised Gentile believers as second-rate Christians (Gal. 2:11-13). Then in verse 14 he mentions what he said to Peter publicly: "If you, though a Jew, live like a Gentile and not like a Jew, how can you force the Gentiles to live like Jews?" In other words, Paul accused the disciple of being a hypocrite. Peter said one thing, but did another. While Peter was saying the "right" thing (uncircumcised Gentile believers are fully Christian), by distancing himself from them he revealed, through his actions, that he thought they were second-class believers.

Did Peter say anything in his own defense? Did he accept Paul's rebuke? Unfortunately, we will never know—at least this side of eternity. What does seem certain, however, is that there was a lot more to the confrontation. And in my opinion, Galatians 2.15, 16 is probably a summary of what else the apostle went on to say to Peter in front of the Gentile and Jewish believers in Antioch.

Seen from this perspective, Paul's statement in Galatians 2:15 makes more sense. Instead of looking at verse 14 as his "own" point of view, it is better to understand it as a statement of a skilled rhetorician who has chosen his words carefully in an attempt to win his opponents over to his own position. Paul attempts to do this by expressing a point of view that he knows his fellow Jews will agree with—the traditional distinction between Jews and Gentiles, the idea that Jews are the elect of God and Gentiles are sinners. To a certain degree, it is correct. God did give His law to the Jews, and they were His covenantal people. But that is not the point that Paul is making. With these words he is trying to gain his opponents' attention by stating something that he knows they will agree with before demonstrating the foolishness of their way of defining the Christian life.

The apostle is convinced that the recognition of Jesus as the promised Messiah has changed everything. The distinction between Jew and Gentile that Peter and the Jews from Jerusalem were advocating was simply not valid. It was a false gospel rooted in human behavior, and Paul was condemning it as he had done earlier (Gal. 1:6-11). How could it be anything else when everything ultimately relies on a person's relationship with Jesus Christ—whether Gentile of Jew? Or as Paul puts it in his own words: "We know that a person is not justified by works of the law but through faith in Jesus Christ, so we also have believed in Christ Jesus, in order to be justified by faith in Christ and not by works of the law, because by works of the law no one will be justified" (Gal. 2:16).

Making Sense of Paul's Theological Lingo

"Justification," "works," "faith"—these three words that Paul repeats several times in Galatians 2:16 make up some of the key words and phrases that he found helpful in explaining the wonderful good news of what God has done for the human race through Jesus' life, death, and resurrection. Anyone who has hung around church for any portion of time also knows that the words are still popular with Christians today. But while they regularly show up in sermons, hymns, and religious songs, some of them have become little more than just spiritual jargon, a kind of special "church talk" with little real meaning attached to them. Paul's use of them, however, gives us the opportunity to consider the rich significance of each of the words, and to see why they have resonated so much with Christians during the past 2,000 years.

Justification

The word "justification" and all its various verbal siblings (just, justice, justified, righteous, and righteousness) was one of Paul's favorite go-to words for explaining the gospel to both Jews and Gentiles. Of the nearly 40 times the verb "to justify" (Greek *dikaioō*) occurs in the New Testament, 27 are in Paul's letters alone—almost 70 percent of its total use. But even more than that, in what may be the first formal written explanation of the gospel (assuming an early date for Galatians), Paul employs "justification" no less than 13 times in his epistle (2:16, 17, 21; 3:6, 8, 11, 21, 24; 5:4, 5), including four references to it in the span of a mere two verses (Gal. 2:16, 17). The frequent use of "justification" in such a short letter as Galatians suggests that it holds the key to understanding the entire epistle itself. So what does it mean to be justified?

Justification is a legal, or forensic, term associated with the judicial proceedings involved in a court of law. It refers to the positive ruling or verdict that a judge pronounces when a person has been determined to be innocent of the charges being brought against him or her. Two passages from the Old Testament illustrate the courtroom imagery connected to it. In Deuteronomy 25:1 God through Moses tells the children of Israel, "If there be a controversy between men, and they come unto judgment, that the judges may judge them; then they shall justify the righteous, and condemn the wicked" (KJV). Proverbs 17:15 uses the identical terminology as part of a warning against corrupt judges. "He who justifies the wicked and he who condemns the righteous are both alike an abomination to the Lord."

Both Old Testament verses mention two legal verdicts side by side. The one verdict is "justification" and the other "condemnation." The fact that the two rulings are diametrically opposed to each other helps us to understand what justification involves. If justification is the opposite of condemnation, then it involves much more than pardon, or the forgiveness of sins. Justification is the positive declaration that a person is "just" or "righteous." In fact, although the words "just" and "righteous" come from two very different English root words, in Greek they actually derive from the same root. To be justified means a person is not merely forgiven but legally declared and counted as "righteous."

The popular television program *CSI: Crime Scene Investigation* offers a more modern illustration of the legal meaning associated with justification. While television audiences have always been fascinated with shows about "cops and robbers," the heroes in *CSI* are not the police, but forensic scientists who are able to solve crimes that otherwise appear to be unsolvable. A forensic scientist is someone who uses science to analyze and present impartial evidence discovered at a scene of a crime that can be used in a court of law. Thus forensic science enables a judge to make a just verdict in a criminal case—to justify the innocent and to condemn the wicked.

Interestingly enough, the word "forensic" comes from the Latin word *"forensis,"* which means "relating to the forum." In Paul's day judicial officials presented criminal charges before local magistrates or even the governor in the city forum—the public square that was the heart of every Greco-Roman town. The accused and the accuser would present speeches setting forth their case, and the person with the best argument and presentation of the evidence would win. The book of Acts makes it clear that Paul was personally acquainted with the legal connotations connected to the word "justification." Time after time, irate Jews dragged him before the local authorities and falsely accused him of malicious intentions (Acts 16:19-23; 17:12-16), and he may have even been tried by the emperor Nero himself (Acts 25:1-12).

When Paul talks about justification, however, he does not have in mind any earthly courtroom. On the contrary, his concern centers on a heavenly throne room where a holy God serves as judge over the inhabitants of the entire world (Rom. 14:10; 2 Cor. 5:10). But here we encounter a problem. How can a holy God—who hates sin—at the same time "justify" or declare sinful human beings as righteous? What can humans do to make sure they will be justified before God and not condemned? This leads to the second key concept that Paul mentions in Galatians 2:15, 16—works of the law.

Works of the Law

How can a person gain God's approval? Conventional wisdom would suggest that the way to get someone's favor is to *do* something good for that person. You have to *earn* it. It happens all the time in society, whether it involves individual relationships or politics. But Paul goes against such conventional wisdom. "We know," he declares, "that a person is not justified by works of the law" (Gal. 2:16; see also Rom. 3:20, 28). The apostle is clear that we can never obtain God's favor by "works of the law," but what exactly does that mean?

The best way to consider what he has in mind by the phrase "works of the law" is to begin with a general assessment of how Paul uses it and how it compares with similar phrases he employs. The phrase "works of the law" (Greek *erga nomou*) occurs eight times in Paul's epistles (see Rom. 3:20, 28; Gal. 2:16; 3:2, 5, 10), and in every case it has a negative connotation. He also uses the word "works" negatively when employed in connection with the flesh (Gal. 5:19) and darkness (Rom. 13:12; Eph. 5:11; cf. of the devil, 1 John 3:8). Lest one mistakenly conclude that Paul is against "works" in general, it is important to note that he often refers to "good works" (Rom. 2:6, 7; 13:3; 2 Cor. 9:8; Eph. 2:10; Phil. 1:6; Col. 1:10; 1 Tim. 5:10; 2 Tim. 2:21; 3:17; Titus 1:16; 3:1) and always in a positive manner. The apostle also speaks positively of the "work of God" (Rom. 14:20) and the "work of Christ" (Phil. 2:30). So whatever issue Paul is addressing, in his mind only the phrase "works of the law" has a negative meaning associated with it.

Surprisingly, he is also the only author in the entire Bible who uses the phrase "works of the law." The expression appears nowhere else in the New Testament, the Old Testament, or even in rabbinic literature from the first two centuries of the Christian Era. For years what appeared to be a unique Pauline expression has puzzled scholars. The lack of any other contemporary use of the phrase led some of them to conclude that by "law" Paul was not referring to God's laws in general, but exclusively to the "identity markers" in Judaism—namely, circumcision, the food regulations, and the Sabbath. Others argued that it was merely his way of talking about legalism since the Hebrew language had no specific word for it.

A significant insight into what Paul meant by the phrase "works of the law" came to light, however, in the late 1980s in a previously unpublished Dead Sea scroll. The Dead Sea scrolls are a collection of writings discovered in 1947 that contain the writings of a conservative sect of Jews known as the Essenes, who flourished in Palestine during the time of Jesus and Paul. The scrolls are of tremendous value because they provide us with the earliest surviving copies of the Hebrew Scriptures as well as valuable insight into the beliefs of a group of Jews living in Jesus' day.

Although written in Hebrew, one of the scrolls contains the exact phrase Paul uses in his letters. The scroll's title is *Miqsat Ma'ase ha-Torah* (commonly referred to as MMT), which can be translated, "Important Works of the Law."[3] The scroll deals with a number of issues based on various biblical laws and is particularly concerned with preventing holy things from being made impure, including several injunctions that warn against contact with Gentiles. At the end of the scroll the author confidently tells his readers that if one obeys these "works of the law," "you will be reckoned righteous" before God. It appears to reflect the exact kind of mentality that Paul fought against in Galatians—the belief that by obedience to God's law a person can win divine favor.

Thus his use of the phrase "works of the law" appears to be similar to what we find in the Dead Sea scrolls. It does not refer exclusively to any one particular law, nor does it undermine the importance of good works performed out of love for God and others. By "works of the law" Paul has in mind any act of obedience to God's law done *in an attempt to earn God's favor*. Legalism. Unlike the author of MMT, the apostle declares that any attempt to gain God's favor by our own good behavior is doomed to failure.

What's so wrong with obedience? Although Paul does not explain it in detail here, the problem is not that obedience is bad or that God's law is somehow insufficient. Rather, the difficulty is with us. Sin has corrupted the human race. As Paul says elsewhere: "All have sinned [in the past], and fall short of the glory of God [in the present]" (Rom. 3:23). We are like a broken violin. Although it might be able to still make some sounds, a damaged violin will never be able to produce the full range of melodious sounds it was originally created to make. The human race is also broken.

So no matter how hard we try to follow God's law, our behavior will never reach the level of perfection necessary for God to declare that we are truly "just" or "righteous." Such a verdict is impossible since His law requires absolute faithfulness in thought and action—not just some of the time, but from our first breath to our last, and not for just some of His commandments, but all of them.

Seen from this perspective, the human problem is not a superficial issue that requires only a few outward modifications here and there. On the contrary, it is something that strikes at the very core of who we are—our identity. For no matter what we do, we still have the same tainted life record that identifies us as sinners.

If our good behavior, our works, are not sufficient to earn God's favor, what hope do we have? This leads us to the final key word Paul uses in Galatians 2:16—faith.

Faith in the Faithfulness of Christ

The key to finding favor with God both now and in the final judgment is not our obedience, but faith. But not just any faith. For Paul faith is not just an abstract concept—it is inseparably connected to Jesus. In fact, the Greek phrase translated twice as "faith in Jesus Christ" in Galatians 2:16 is far richer than any rendering can really encompass (see also Rom. 3:22, 26; Gal. 3:22; Eph. 3:12; Phil. 3:9). In Greek the phrase literally means "the faith of Jesus" or "the faithfulness of Jesus." It reveals the powerful contrast the apostle makes between the works of the law and the work of Christ accomplished on our behalf. For Paul, the primary emphasis is not *our* faith in Jesus, but Jesus' faithfulness. Thus the issue is not *our* works versus *our* faith—that would almost make our faith meritorious, which it is not. Rather, faith is only the conduit by which we take hold of Christ. We are justified, not on the basis of *our* faith, but on the basis of *Christ's faithfulness*.

Jesus did what Israel as a nation and every individual Israelite failed to do—He was faithful to God in every moment of His life. Though tempted in "all points . . . like as we are" (Heb. 4:15, KJV), Jesus never once wavered or gave way to sin. He lived the perfect life that God's law required, and as the second Adam He rewrote the history of the human race (Rom. 5:18, 19). He offers to us today that new history—a new identity, one marked not by sin, failure, and defeat, but by purity, righteousness, and victory.

Our only hope resides in Christ's faithfulness. Instead of trusting in our own faulty behavior to somehow win God's favor, we are called by Paul to put our faith, our complete trust, in Christ's faithfulness. It is only on the basis of God's work in Christ that sinners can be justified in God's sight. As one author puts it: "We believe in Christ, not that we might be justified by that belief, but that we might be justified by his faith(fulness) to God."[4] An early Syriac translation from the fifth century known as the Peshitta conveys Paul's original meaning well. It reads: "For we know that a man is not justified from the works of the law, but by the *faith of Jesus* the Messiah, and we believe *in* him, *in Jesus the Messiah,* in order that *from his faith,* that of the Messiah, we might be justified, and not by the works of the law."[5]

The faith or belief that Paul calls us to express in Christ is not some kind of feeling or attitude that one day we decide to have just because God requires it. On the contrary, genuine biblical faith is always a response to Him. It originates in a heart touched with a sense of gratitude and love for His goodness. That is why when the Bible talks about someone's faith, that faith is always a response to some initiative God has taken. In the case of Abraham, for example, faith is his response to the fantastic promises God makes to him (Gen. 12:1-4). In the New Testament, however, true, genuine, saving faith is ultimately rooted in our personal realization that in Christ's life, death, and resurrection, God offers to us a new identity—the very identity of his Son.

The Ingredients of Genuine Faith

Many people like to define faith as belief. But such a definition is problematic, since in Greek the word for faith is simply the noun form of the verb "to believe." To use one form to define the other is basically like saying faith is to have faith—that doesn't help us.

A careful examination of Scripture reveals that faith comprises two key components. First, it involves not only knowledge about God but a mental assent or acceptance of that knowledge. That is one reason that having an accurate picture of God is so important. Distorted ideas about His character can actually make it more difficult for people to have faith. But an intellectual assent to the gospel is not enough, for "even the demons believe" in that sense.

True faith also affects the way a person lives. In Romans 1:5 Paul talks about the "obedience of faith." The apostle does not mean that obedience is the same as faith. Rather, true faith shapes a person's whole life—not just the mind. It involves trust and commitment—not simply to some list of rules, but to our Lord and Savior, Jesus Christ.

One of the main accusations against Paul was that his gospel of justification by faith encouraged people to sin (see Rom. 3:8; 6:1). No doubt his opponents reasoned that if people do not have to keep the law to be accepted by God, why should they be concerned with how they live at all?

Paul finds such reasoning simply preposterous. Accepting Christ by faith is not something trivial, neither is it a game of heavenly make-believe whereby God simply counts a person as righteous without any real change in how he or she lives. On the contrary, to accept Christ by faith is extremely radical. It represents a complete union with Christ—union in both His death and resurrection. Spiritually speaking, the apostle says that we are crucified with Christ. As a result, our old sinful ways rooted in selfishness are finished (Rom. 6:5-14). We have made a radical break with the past. Everything is new (2 Cor. 5:17). Also we have been raised to a new life in Christ. The resurrected Christ lives within us daily, making us more and more like Himself. While many have often mistakenly pitted Paul and James against each other, in context they both agree that faith without works is dead (cf. James 2:26; 1:22; Rom. 2:13).

Faith in Christ, therefore, is not a pretext for sin, but a call to a much deeper, richer relationship with Christ than could ever be found in a solely law-based religion.

Our Identity From God's Perspective

Many people love mirrors—and can't seem to live without having one nearby. While mirrors can certainly be helpful, they are not always all that great. Instead of giving us a clear picture of ourselves, on a certain level they actually present more of a distorted picture of reality. If you think about it, all mirrors really do is make us think about ourselves and point out all our imperfections. Whenever we look in a mirror, we always find something that we need to fix. Can you think of a time that even the quickest glance in the mirror did not call for some sort of straightening or adjusting action? Mirrors really remind us of all the ways that we don't measure up.

Spiritually speaking, mirrors can be dangerous if all they do is teach us to look at ourselves in light of our own identity. Rather than staring at ourselves in the mirror and beholding all our faults and failures, we are called by God to look at ourselves and our fellow brothers and sisters in Christ from His perspective. When He looks at us, He does not see all the imperfections we so readily detect in each other and ourselves. Instead He views the spotless life of His Son, for what is true of Christ is true of all those who place their faith in His faithfulness.

[1] T. Wright, *Paul for Everyone*, p. 24.

[2] *Ibid.* (Italics supplied.)

[3] Martin Abegg, "Paul, 'Works of the Law,' and MMT," *Biblical Archaeology Review,* November-December 1994, pp. 52-55, 82.

[4] J. McRay, *Paul: His Life and Teachings,* p. 355.

[5] Author's translation.

CHAPTER 5

Faith Alone in Christ

Startling news rocked the evangelical world on May 5, 2007, when Francis Beckwith, president of the Evangelical Theological Society, resigned his position, disavowed his connections to Protestantism, and formally joined the Roman Catholic Church. To the average person Beckwith's decision probably did not seem that significant. People switch back and forth between churches all the time, so what makes his story so newsworthy? But anyone acquainted with the history of Martin Luther and the rise of Protestantism realizes that Beckwith's decision to become a Roman Catholic was not as simple as a person transferring from a Baptist to a Methodist church. Although Protestants and Catholics share some common beliefs, many significant theological differences separate them—for example, the Roman Catholic veneration of Mary, the inclusion of writings from the Apocrypha as part of the Bible, the belief in purgatory, prayers for the dead, and the doctrine of papal infallibility. But what made Beckwith's departure from Protestantism so unsettling to evangelical Christians was the reason he gave for his decision.

In an interview with *Christianity Today* Beckwith stated that the primary factor that led him to become a Roman Catholic was that he no longer agreed with the core doctrine of Protestantism—the belief that justification is by faith *alone*.[1] He struggled with the idea that faith and faith alone was all that was necessary for a person to be right with God. In his own words, Beckwith said that he found Catholicism more attractive because it "frames the Christian life as one in which you must exercise virtue. . . . As an evangelical, even when I talked about sanctification and wanted to practice it, it seemed as if I didn't have a good enough incentive to do so."[2] From his perspective, the belief that faith alone reconciles humans to the Father gives too much significance to faith and not enough emphasis to the necessity of obedience.

Beckwith is not the first person to be uncomfortable with the way that the teaching of justification by faith has led some evangelicals to downplay the importance of obedience in the life of the believer. Since not all forms of Protestant Christianity minimize following God's law, one can only assume that Beckwith's decision to walk away from Protestantism was ultimately a reaction to a distorted view of justification by faith. Because Beckwith was formerly a Baptist, it seems logical to conclude that he was reacting to the typical Baptist belief of "once saved, always saved." While emphasizing the assurance of salvation in Christ alone, the teaching skews the biblical teaching of the perseverance of the saints and has often lured some to the dangerous conclusion that obedience to God is optional. It appears that Beckwith's decision led him from one doctrinal error into another.

While his perspective is a valid criticism of some forms of contemporary evangelical Christianity (cf. James 2:14-26), it is certainly not an accurate portrayal of Paul's teaching on justification by faith. Salvation is by faith in Christ alone, but faith always leads to obedience—not because a person has to obey to be saved, but because a believer has already been saved. Like many Christians today, the apostle's opponents in Galatia had become confused on the point. They mistakenly believed that he was overemphasizing the role of faith in salvation, and that he was not placing nearly enough stress on the necessity of obedience in the life of the believer (cf. Gal. 2:17, 18; Rom. 2:8; 3:31; 6:1).

Up until this point in Galatians Paul has been defending the divine origin of his gospel and demonstrating that even the apostles endorse his message. After having explained that justification is by faith and not the works of the law (Gal. 2:15-21), he knows that his opponents will immediately begin to raise objections about the all-sufficiency of faith. So in anticipation of their protest, he demonstrates in Galatians 2:1-14 why faith alone is the only reliable means of securing God's favor. He attempts to do it in two ways. First he approaches the issue from the perspective of personal experience—the personal experience of the Galatians and then to the experience of Abraham, the ancestor of the Jewish race (Gal. 3:1-9). Finally Paul directs their attention to the testimony of Scripture on the issue (verses 10-14).

The Experience of the Galatians (Gal. 3:1-6)

His opening words in Galatians 3 illustrate how concerned (and completely baffled) he was by the Galatians' about-face on the gospel. Several

47

modern translations have tried to capture the sense of his words in verse 1, but none equals the utter amazement conveyed in J. B. Phillips: "Dear idiots of Galatia." While we might be a little uncomfortable with the candor of the Phillips translation, it actually reflects Paul's original terminology quite well. The word he used in Greek is *anoetoi*, which literally means "mindless." What were the Galatians thinking by relying on their own behavior for salvation? The problem, as the apostle saw it, was that they were not thinking at all. In fact, they were behaving so foolishly that he wondered if someone had cast a spell over them. Such strong terminology from Paul was, no doubt, an attempt to awaken the Galatians from their spiritual stupor.

Hoping to help the Galatians come to their senses, Paul reminded them in verse 2 of how they had first come to understand and accept the gospel. "Did you receive the Spirit by works of the law [i.e., by obeying God's law to earn His favor] or by hearing with faith [i.e., believing the gospel]?" Paul did not approach them with some sort of complicated formula for salvation. His message had been simple and straightforward. "It was before your eyes that Jesus Christ was publicly portrayed as crucified" (verse 1). The word translated "portrayed" literally means "placarded" or "painted," and it was used to describe all public proclamations. How could they forget it? The cross was such a central part of Paul's gospel presentation that the Galatians had, in effect, seen Christ crucified (1 Cor. 1:23; 2:2). The apostle's message had centered, not on something the Galatians had to do to earn God's favor, but on simply accepting by faith what Christ had already done for them at Calvary.

The apostle next asked a series of questions designed to get the Galatians to contrast their current experience with the simplicity of how they first came to faith in Christ. "Are you so foolish? Having begun by the Spirit, are you now being perfected by the flesh? . . . Does he who supplies the Spirit to you and works miracles among you do so by works of the law, or by hearing with faith . . . ?" (Gal. 3:3-5).

The answer to each question is the same: no single aspect of the Galatians' Christian experience had its basis in something they had done to earn it. Their salvation was completely because of God's initiative. Paul had come to Galatia preaching the gospel of the crucified and risen Messiah. The Galatians had accepted the apostle's message, placed their trust in Christ, and received God's promised Spirit. All this was God's free gift to them. They had done nothing to earn it. Nor had Paul required them to be first circumcised or to keep God's law. They had come to

Christ just as they were, and He had accepted them—not because they deserved it, but because of His great love for them (Eph. 2:4). And even the miracles they had witnessed in their life as Christians were not of their own doing—they too were solely the work of God's Spirit that had been given to them as a gift (Acts 2:38). Thus from start to finish, everything they had experienced as Christians was a gift from God. What would make them think that now they had to rely upon their own behavior?

It seems that part of the problem was that the Galatians had failed to preserve the distinction between justification and sanctification. As we have seen previously, justification refers to the act whereby God legally pronounces a sinner to be just or righteous in His sight because of what *He has already done for them* in Christ. Justification is our title to heaven. Sanctification, however, refers to the enabling power of God's Spirit that begins to work *in us* the very moment we are justified. Thus sanctification is not the means by which we earn the right to enter into heaven it is the way that God fits us to live in heaven. It is the process by which God makes real in our experience what is already true of us by faith in Christ.

While both aspects of salvation should be present in the believer's life, they must come in the proper sequence and never be confused. The Christian life begins with justification by faith—believing that God accepts us not because we are worthy, but because Christ, our substitute, is worthy. What Jesus did for us in His life, death, and resurrection is the sole basis of our salvation. It cannot and need not be improved on. Then once we have accepted God's gift of salvation by faith, His Spirit begins to work in our lives, enabling us to become more and more like Christ. But the work God's Spirit does in our lives does not contribute one iota to our salvation. It merely demonstrates that we have surrendered our lives to Christ.

Although written nearly 2,000 years ago, Paul's counsel to the Galatians contains a fundamental truth about the Christian life that we would be wise never to forget. No matter how God's Spirit may transform our lives, no matter how we may grow in spiritual knowledge or ability, the basis of our acceptance with Christ never changes—it is faith in what *God* has done for us in Christ.

The Experience of Abraham (Gal. 3:7-9)

Paul now turns his attention from the personal experience of the Galatians to that of Abraham. The patriarch was a central figure in Judaism. Not only was he the father of the Jewish race, but also in Paul's day Jews looked to him as the prototype of what it meant to be a genuine Jew. What was the nature of Abraham's personal experience with God?

No doubt Paul's opponents in Galatia felt that the defining characteristic of Abraham's experience with God was his obedience. Had Abraham not forsaken his homeland and family, and even consented to sacrifice his son in obedience to God's command? And, as Paul's adversaries were surely more than glad to emphasize, Abraham had even willingly submitted in obedience to the rite of circumcision.

An interesting confirmation that Jews living in the first centuries B.C. and A.D. looked in admiration at Abraham as an ideal example of a life of obedience appear in an ancient Jewish book entitled Jubilees. Originally written in Hebrew around the middle of the second century B.C., Jubilees purports to be an account told by an angel to Moses during the 40 days he spent on Mount Sinai (see Ex. 24:18). Moses learned the story of the children of Israel from Creation to the Exodus with a particular focus on the obedience of Abraham. Although most of the stories in Jubilees come from the Bible, they often receive an unusual twist. In the case of Abraham, the author also introduces a number of apocryphal tales about how devoted and obedient Abraham was even as a little child. They seem to illustrate that God chose him because he was so obedient. The writer also goes out of his way to whitewash some of the more sordid tales from Abraham's life. For example, in the incident in which Pharaoh took Abraham's wife, Sarah, the author conveniently omits the part about Abraham lying about her identity as his wife. In this case Abraham's behavior needed a little help.

The book of Jubilees also gives additional insight into the importance some Jews placed on circumcision. In it the angel tells Moses that in the future the sons of Israel will turn away from obeying the law of circumcision. As a result, "great wrath from the Lord will be upon the sons of Israel" "because they have made themselves like the gentiles. . . . There is therefore for them no forgiveness or pardon so that they might be pardoned and forgiven from all the sins of this eternal error."[3] The passage sounds like something that Paul's opponents would have agreed with themselves.

The apostle, however, turns the tables on his opponents by appealing to Abraham not merely as an example of the all-sufficiency of faith, but as the fundamental basis of his entire gospel. The experience of Abraham is so fundamental to Paul's understanding of the role of faith in the believer's life that he mentions him no less than nine times in Galatians.

First Paul introduces Abraham as part of a quotation from Genesis 15:6. Abraham "believed the Lord, and he counted to him as righteousness." Here it is important to remember that the word "faith" and the verb "to believe" come from the same root in Greek. God counted or regarded Abraham as righteous because of the man's faith. The word "counted" or "reckoned" is a metaphor drawn from the business world. It means to "credit" or "to place something to an individual's account." Paul not only uses it of Abraham in Galatians 3:6, but another 11 times in connection with the patriarch in the fourth chapter of Romans (see Rom. 4:3, 4, 5, 6, 8, 9, 10, 11, 22, 23, 24).

According to Paul's metaphor, what God credits to our accounts is righteousness—the very thing we lack in ourselves. On what basis does He reckon us as righteous? It surely cannot be our obedience, as Paul's opponents claimed. For no matter what may be said about Abraham's obedience, Scripture says that it was because of his faith that God counted him as righteous. Scripture is clear. Abraham's obedience was not the ground of his justification, but the result. Moreover, God had counted him as righteous some 15 years before he was even circumcised!

In fact, God's promise to Abraham in Genesis 12:3 makes it abundantly clear that from the very beginning He did not intend His covenant to be solely for the Jews. "In you all the families of the earth shall be blessed" (Gen. 12:3). And to make sure that Abraham and his descendants did not forget that they were to bring God's plan of salvation to the rest of the world, the book of Genesis repeats the same promise four more times (Gen. 18:18; 22:18; 26:4; 28:14).

The basis of God's covenant with Abraham centered on the divine promise to him. In the span of three short verses in Genesis 12:1-3, God says to Abraham four times, "I will." "I will show you a land." "I will make you a great nation." "I will bless you." And finally, "I will bless those who bless you." The divine promises to Abraham are amazing because they are completely one-sided. Notice how the Lord does all the promising and requires Abraham to promise nothing in return. It is the opposite of how most people try to relate to God. We usually promise God that we will serve Him if He will do something for us in return. But that is legalism. God did not ask Abraham to promise anything. Instead, the Lord asks him to accept His promises by faith. Of course, that was no easy task. Abraham had to learn to trust completely in God and not in himself, something that goes against all worldly wisdom.

Faith was the defining mark of Abraham's life. And even though he questioned and wavered from time to time, what astonishing faith he had in God's promises. It was his faith in the divine promise that prompted him to leave the comforts and conveniences of Ur of the Chaldees to head across the world to a land he had never even seen. And although Sarah and he were long past childbearing years, he still believed that God could do what was medically impossible—provide them with their own biological son (Rom. 4:19-21; Heb. 11:11, 12). When God's promise seemed to tarry, Abraham continued to believe year after year that the Lord would fulfill His promise no matter what. And even when God commanded him to sacrifice his promised son, Isaac, Abraham was convinced that God would surely bring him back to life because the Lord would never break His promise (Heb. 11:17-19).

Abraham was obedient, but his relationship with God was not rooted in his own obedience. If it had been, the mistakes he made throughout his life would have quickly disqualified him. The patriarch's obedience was only a by-product of his faith. He found favor in God's sight because he was willing to trust completely in God's promises and not in his own abilities or behavior. For this reason the experience of Abraham contains the essence of what the gospel is all about—complete faith in God's promise to do for Abraham and his descendants what they could not do for themselves.

The Testimony of Scripture (Gal. 3:10-14)

While the experience of the Galatians and even of Abraham himself implies that faith is sufficient for salvation, Paul goes on to argue that the Hebrew Scriptures themselves explicitly teach that human obedience to God's law will never be enough to merit salvation. The apostle does this by alluding to several verses from the books of Deuteronomy and Leviticus.

- "Cursed be everyone who does not abide by all things written in the Book of the Law, and do them" (Gal. 3:10; Deut. 27:26).
- "The one who does them shall live by them" (Gal. 3:12; Lev. 18:5).
- "Cursed is everyone who is hanged on a tree" (Gal. 3:13; Deut. 21:22, 23).

At first glance the logic behind Paul's collection of Old Testament verses and his rapid-fire presentation of them in Galatians 3:10-14 may seem rather obscure. In fact, some might even be tempted to charge him with an ill-advised use of proof texting—that is, bringing together disparate passages whose original context share no genuine connection. But even if he is not guilty of proof texting, how do they indicate that human obedience is not a prerequisite for salvation?[4] If anything, they seem to emphasize that obedience *is* necessary. What exactly is Paul saying?

While proof texting is often an illegitimate hermeneutical exercise, we can hardly charge Paul with a careless or irresponsible use of Scripture. As a Jewish rabbi he knew the Hebrew scriptures, and he knew them well. Careful examination of his quotations even indicates that he was familiar with them both in Hebrew and in the Greek translation known as the Septuagint (abbreviated as LXX). Though it is difficult to know exactly how many hundreds of times he quotes or alludes to the Scriptures, we find references to them scattered throughout all his letters, with the sole exception of Titus and Philemon, his two shortest epistles.

In the case of his quotations in Galatians 3:10-14, Paul knows Scripture well enough not to have merely thrown together a bunch of disparate texts with no logical connection. On the contrary, his argument is quite logical and the quotations he uses to develop it are linked together by a series of verbal parallels. The two passages in Deuteronomy each contain the word "cursed," and the passage from Leviticus and Habakkuk share "will live." In addition, Leviticus 18:5 and Deuteronomy 27:26 also employ the word translated into English as "to do." Such verbal parallels allow him to interpret each passage of Scripture in relation to the other.[5] And the logic that he finds in these passages seems to develop along the following lines:

- Law is based on the principle of *doing,* not on believing (Gal. 3:12).
- Law requires perfect obedience to all of its precepts all of the time (verse 10).
- Failure to do all of the law all of the time brings a person under the law's curse (verse 10).
- Conclusion: No one can be justified before God by the law because no one (except Jesus) has ever fulfilled the entire law. Therefore, *everyone* is under the law's curse.[6]

Paul's bold words in Galatians 3:10 no doubt stunned his opponents. They certainly did not think themselves to be under a curse—if anything, they expected to be blessed for their obedience.

Although the picture he paints is rather bleak, all is not hopeless. Two beacons of hope lighten the dark sky. The first ray of hope occurs in a quotation from Habakkuk 2:4 that the apostle tucks right in the midst of the verses he cites to demonstrate that no human being can hope to find life by keeping the law. Habakkuk, a prophet of God who lived during a time that there seemed little hope for the survival of Israel, proclaimed that the only way to life was faith. "The righteous shall live by his faith" (Hab. 2:4). This passage, which Paul also cites in Romans 1:17, views faith as both the way to righteousness and the way to life. As such it characterizes a person's relationship with God from start to finish.

The second beacon of hope comes as a remedy to the curse of the law announced in verse 10. "Christ," Paul says, "redeemed us from the curse of the law by becoming a curse for us—for it is written, 'Cursed is everyone who is hanged on a tree'" (Gal. 3:13). Here the apostle introduces us to yet another metaphor to explain what God has done for us in Christ. Christ has "redeemed" us.

Today the word "redeemed" is largely a religious word. But that was not the case in Paul's day. In his time the dominant use of the word was secular. It literally meant "to buy back." The ancients used it of the ransom price paid to secure the release of individuals being held as hostages, or the amount required to free a person from slavery. Likely building on Jesus' own use of the word in relation to His ministry (Mark 10:45; Matt. 20:28), Paul employs the same metaphor to explain what Christ has done for us. Since the wages of sin is death (Rom. 6:23), the curse of the law was ultimately a death sentence. Jesus paid the penalty of our sin by becoming our sinbearer (1 Cor. 6:20; 7:23). Voluntarily He took our curse upon Himself and suffered in our behalf the full wages of sin (2 Cor. 5:21).

Paul cites Deuteronomy 21:23 as scriptural proof for what he has just said about the cross. Jewish custom regarded a person as under God's curse if after execution their bodies were hung upon a tree. Many saw Jesus' death on the cross as such an example (Acts 5:30; 1 Peter 2:24), the reason the cross was a stumbling block for so many Jews. They could not fathom the idea that the Messiah would be accursed by God. But that was exactly the divine plan. The curse Christ bore was not His own, but ours.

Christ has done for us what we could never have accomplished ourselves. No matter how sincere or faithful we have determined to be in our lives, we have all fallen short in many ways. What wonderful news to contemplate that our salvation is not rooted in what we have done, or have to do, but in what God has already accomplished. As Archbishop William Temple once said: "The only thing of my very own which I contribute to my redemption is the sin from which I need to be redeemed."[7] Whereas the law says "Do" and then condemns us for having fallen short, the gospel says "Done" and then gives us the power to live a life of holiness. Thus all we have, we have received from Christ. He and He alone deserves all our praise.

"How vast the benefits divine which we in Christ possess!
We are redeemed from guilt and shame and called to holiness.
But not for works which we have done, or shall hereafter do,
Hath God decreed on sinful men salvation to bestow.
The glory, Lord, from first to last, is due to Thee alone;
Aught to ourselves we dare not take, or rob Thee of Thy crown."[8]

---

[1] During the past three decades Roman Catholic scholars have dialogued with Protestants in an attempt to correct prejudices and false stereotypes, and to promote unity on common moral issues. One of the issues discussed has been the dividing issue of justification by faith. A meeting between the Pontifical Council for Promoting Christian Unity and the Lutheran World Federation published a document in 1999 entitled *Joint Declaration on the Doctrine of Justification* (*JDDJ*). In it Lutherans and Roman Catholics agreed on the following definition of justification: "Together we confess: By grace alone, in faith in Christ's saving work and not because of any merit on our part, we are accepted by God and receive the Holy Spirit, who renews our hearts while equipping and calling us to good works" (http://www.vatican.va/roman_curia/pontifical_councils/chrstuni/documents/rc_pc_chrstuni_doc_31101999_cath-luth-annex_en.html). The World Methodist Council also officially adopted the statement in 2006.

While the document has certainly promoted greater mutual understanding, it has not, contrary to some claims, resolved the historic difference of opinion on justification between traditional Protestantism and Roman Catholicism. Although there is nothing objectionable in what is stated in the *JDDJ*, the difficulty resides in what it does *not* say. Belief in grace alone and faith in Christ has never been an issue of contention between Protestants and Catholics. The dividing issue has been whether faith "alone" is sufficient. Roman Catholicism continues to proclaim that while faith is important, it by itself is not sufficient for justification. Rather, good works empowered by the Spirit are a necessary prerequisite for justification. Salvation in Roman Catholic theology is rooted in faith plus works, not faith alone.

While Protestants and Catholics certainly share much in common and should continue to dialogue and work together in areas in which there is mutual agreement, like Paul in Galatians we must continue to point to the all-sufficiency of faith alone in Christ as the only prerequisite for salvation.

[2] David Neff, "Q&A: Francis Beckwith," *Christianity Today* [cited May 29, 2009]. Online: http://www.christianitytoday.com/ct/2007/mayweb-only/119-33.0.html.

[3] Jubilees 15:33, in James H. Charlesworth, ed., *The Old Testament Pseudepigrapha*, Anchor Bible Reference Library (New York: Doubleday, 1985), vol. 2, p. 87.

[4] David K. Huttar, *Galatians: The Gospel According to Paul* (Christian Publications, 2001), p. 83.

[5] Frank Matera, *Galatians*, Sacra Pagina Series (Collegeville, Minn.: Liturgical Press,

1992), vol. 9, p. 121.

⁶ Huttar, p. 83.

⁷ As quoted in John Stott, *Through the Bible Through the Year* (Grand Rapids: Baker Books, 2006), p. 349.

⁸ Augustus M. Toplady, "How Vast the Benefits Divine," *Gospel Magazine,* 1774 [cited May 29, 2009]. Online: http://nethymnal.org/htm/h/v/hvasttbd.htm.

CHAPTER 6

The Priority of the Promise

Where did she want to be buried? Who was the father of her daughter? And who would become the guardian of her daughter's vast inheritance? Such questions created a legal nightmare and led to a media frenzy that captivated tabloid headlines and dominated the attention of cable television news shows and talk radio for weeks in 2007. The source of all this mess was the sad and tragic death of Anna Nicole Smith, the actress and model who died from an accidental drug overdose without ever having updated her will to account for the birth of her daughter, Danielynn, and the subsequent death of her son, Daniel.

Everyone connected to the case—and even those not involved with it—seemed to have a different opinion about what Anna Nicole Smith would have wanted. Some claimed she would have desired to be buried near her family in Texas, others argued for Los Angeles, and still others claimed it would have been to be buried beside her son's grave in the Bahamas. And then in a rather bizarre turn of events at least five different men claimed to have possibly fathered her daughter, Danielynn. Such sensational drama contributed to a media circus unlike anything the legal world had seen in years. In the end the only thing that all the disputing parties seemed to be able to agree on was how *different* the whole situation would have been if Anna Nicole Smith had only left an updated will clearly stating what she wanted to happen upon her death.

In stark contrast to all the uncertainty that surrounded the wishes of Anna Nicole Smith at her death, there is, fortunately, no question about what God desires for His people. God's Word is sure and unchanging. And according to Paul's letter to the Galatians, the Lord has made it plain in His dealings with Abraham that salvation is by faith and faith alone. Human obedience to God's law does not contribute anything to a person's acceptance before Him. The apostle's strong insistence on faith leads to some very important questions, however. If faith is indeed the end-all in terms of acceptance before God, why did He give the children of Israel His law in the first place? Did it not signify that He had replaced, nullified, or at least altered the covenant He had made with Abraham 430 years earlier? What is the proper relationship between faith and the law of God? Paul's opponents in Galatia were wondering the same kinds of things. In Galatians 3:15-20 the apostle makes one final argument in favor of the sufficiency of faith alone, and then proceeds to tackle the questions about the relationship between faith and the law.

The Galatians as "Brothers"

Paul begins his comments in Galatians 3:10 with a word that we might easily overlook as insignificant, but is actually worthy of our attention. He addresses the Galatians as "brothers" (verse 15). Why does the word deserve our attention? Up until this point in Galatians we might be tempted to view his relationship with the Galatians as completely hostile, if not downright hateful. After all, the apostle left out the word of thanksgiving that customarily begins his letters, pronounced a curse on anyone who preaches a different gospel, and then referred to the Galatians as mindless and bewitched (Gal. 3:1). Although he was certainly upset, we would gravely misunderstand the nature of his relationship with the Galatians if we failed to note that he also refers to them as "brothers." And it is no slip of the tongue on his part either. He addresses them with the term of endearment a total of nine times (Gal. 1:11; 3:15; 4:12, 28, 31; 5:11, 13; 6:1, 18) and practically comes to tears in his appeal to them (Gal. 4:12-16, 19, 20). His repeated reference to the Galatians as his brothers indicates that in spite of their differences, he still believes a close relationship exists between them. They are not his enemies—they are family.

We must filter all of his passionate and fiery terminology through this perspective. Paul is involved in an in-house quarrel between siblings. And although his culture was certainly more candid than we might be comfortable with today, it is still important to remember that a quarrel between siblings is vastly different from a disagreement between two unrelated individuals. Though the words may be the same in both cases, the impact is radically different. What gets exchanged in a squabble among family members is always softened by a shared relationship. When someone else says those same words, however, that cushion is not there. It is no longer about "us"—it is about "them." If we fail to interpret Paul's dispute with the Galatians from within this context, we run the risk not only of distorting

More parent-child

58

our picture of Paul, but of turning Galatians into little more than a harangue.

God's Unchangeable Promise (Gal. 3:15-18)

In a final attempt to demonstrate to the Galatians that God's covenant with Abraham and all his descendants rested on faith apart from works of the law, Paul draws on an example taken from everyday life. "Once a person's will has been ratified," he says, "no one adds to it or annuls it" (Gal. 3:15, NRSV).

The terminology and logic of Paul's illustration has puzzled translators and commentators alike. The word translated as "will" in Greek (*diathēkē*) can also be accurately translated as "covenant." Either rendering is equally possible. One can notice this difference by comparing how different translations of the Bible handle the verse. The problem, however, is that there is a vast difference between a "covenant" and a "will." A covenant is typically a mutual agreement between two or more people, often called a contract or treaty. A will is the declaration of a single person. Paul's reference to Abraham in the preceding verses might suggest that the context indicates that "covenant" is the word he had in mind. It is true that the Septuagint, the Greek translation of the Hebrew Scriptures, often uses the word *diathēkē* that way. The difficulty is that the Greek word *diathēkē* always refers to a person's final will and testament in secular sources.[1] Thus the evidence in favor of either word is basically split equally.

So which is it? Is Paul's illustration about a "covenant" or a "will"? The answer is that the apostle appears to have both concepts in mind.

While the word for covenant and will are very different in English, they are not so unrelated in Greek. The Greek translation of the Old Testament never renders the Hebrew word (Heb. *berît*) for God's covenant with Abraham with the Greek word used for mutual agreements (*synthēkē*) or contracts. Instead the Septuagint employs the word typically used for a testament or a will (*diathēkē*). Why? Likely because the translators recognized that God's covenant with Abraham was not like a treaty between two individuals who made mutually binding promises to each other. On the contrary, God's covenant was based on nothing other than His own good pleasure. It has no string of ifs, ands, or buts attached to it. Abraham was simply to take the Lord at His word.

Paul appears to have picked up on this double meaning of the word for will and covenant, and he uses it to highlight specific features of God's covenant with Abraham. Like a human will, for example, God's covenant concerns a specific beneficiary—Abraham and his offspring (Gen. 12:1-5; Gal. 3:16). It also involves an inheritance (Gen. 13:15; 17:8; Rom. 4:13). But most important to Paul is the unchanging nature of the divine covenant. If a legally ratified will cannot be altered or modified in any way once the testator dies, God's covenantal promises to Abraham are all the more immutable. His covenant is a promise (Gal. 3:16), and by no means is He a promise breaker (Isa. 46:11; Heb. 6:18).

The inviolable covenant that God made with Abraham is not merely a matter of antiquity, however. In one sense, it actually spans all time since it was not limited to Abraham alone, but it also applied to his offspring (Gen. 17:1-8). The reference to Abraham's offspring evokes a parenthetical comment by Paul regarding the meaning of the word "offspring." "It does not say, 'And to offsprings,' referring to many, but referring to one, 'And to your offspring,' who is Christ" (Gal. 3:16). As is the case in English, the word for "offspring" in Hebrew and Greek can have a collective sense attached to it, though it is actually singular in number. The fact that "offspring" is singular suggests to Paul that it is a reference to Christ as the true, single descendant of Abraham and the ultimate beneficiary through whom God would bless all the nations of the world.

While Paul's reasoning may seem like a case of grammatical hairsplitting, it not only demonstrates his attention to the details of Scripture, but reveals a significant insight into his understanding of the promise God gave to Abraham. From Paul's perspective not a single one of Abraham's literal descendants ever really inherited the full extent of the promises that the Lord made to Abraham (cf. Heb. 11:39). It is only in Christ, the true seed of Abraham, that *all* the nations of the earth have been blessed. As Donald Guthrie notes: "The real blessing which has come upon Jew and Gentile alike has come only in Christ. He is the Seed of Abraham *par excellence*, and all who are in him are equally Abraham's sons."[2] For this reason Christ is all that really matters, for as Paul says in Galatians 3:29, "If you are Christ's, then you are Abraham's offspring, heirs according to promise."

Not wanting the Galatians to miss the main point of his comparison of God's covenant to a person's final will and testament, the apostle states it plainly. "This is what I mean: the law, which came 430 years afterward, does not annul a covenant previously ratified by God, so as to make the promise void" (verse 17). The Galatians can say all they want about the law, but the fact is that God never related to Abraham on its basis. The Lord gave it to the children of Israel much later. Faith was all that He required in the covenant He made with Abraham and his descendants. To say that the law is now a requirement to receive God's promise would mean that the Lord defaulted on His promise. Frank Matera nicely summaries the rationale behind Paul's thinking.

"It is inconceivable for Paul that the Law could annul the promise or act as a codicil to God's testament. If it did, then God would be capricious. If the Law annulled the promise, then God would be unfaithful to Himself, as well as to Abraham. No, the Law was a latecomer; it was given at Sinai 430 years after God legally ratified His testament with Abraham. As important and as holy as the Law is, therefore, it cannot add to or annul what God has already promised by solemn oath to Abraham."[3]

Why Did God Give the Law? (Gal. 3:19, 20)

Paul anticipates the question his opponents were probably jumping out of their seats to ask. "If God's covenantal promises to Abraham were entirely unaffected by the law, why did God give the law in the first place?" The apostle replies, "It was added because of transgressions, until the offspring should come to whom the promise had been made" (verse 19). What exactly does he mean? His answer is so terse it raises a number of important—and debated—questions that we need to answer before we can really understand what he is saying. What law was added? Why was it "added"? And for how long? We will consider each question in order.

1. What law was added?

Paul says the law was added, but what exactly is he talking about? Answering this question is not as easy as it may seem at first, since the word "law" can refer to a variety of things in his letters. The word "law" occurs more than 100 times in his epistles. Paul can use it to refer to God's will for His people, the Pentateuch (Rom. 3:21), a specific book in the Old Testament (1 Cor. 14:21), the entire Old Testament (Rom. 3:10-19; 5:13), or even just a general principle (Rom. 7:21). And if those were not enough options to deal with, some scholars have claimed that the law in Galatians refers only to the ceremonial laws involving sacrifices and offerings. And still others have identified it with the moral law in particular. What are we to make of this?

Interestingly enough, the question about the identity of the law in Galatians was a hotly debated question among Seventh-day Adventists around the end of the nineteenth century. In fact, it generated a number of controversial debates and articles, and even spilled over into the publication of several books that dwelt entirely on the topic.[4] (If you think this

61

section is tedious, just imagine reading a couple hundred pages on it!)

The traditional interpretation among early Adventist ministers and evangelists had been that the "added law" referred to the ceremonial law, and that law was ultimately done away with by Christ's sacrifice on Calvary. They saw confirmation of their interpretation in the belief that the word "until" in verse 19 indicates this law was only temporary in duration. It proved to be a popular understanding since it helped Adventists demonstrate that the moral law of God—and in particular the Sabbath—had not been abolished at Calvary. In opposition to the traditional view, a younger group of ministers argued that the moral law made far more sense of Paul's overall argument in Galatians. The debate ended up becoming so contentious that Ellen White had to rebuke both groups for their lack of Christian civility. As it turns out, both sides largely missed Paul's point.

The identity of the law in Galatians needs to be seen in light of his overall message in Galatians. Although the apostle is arguing against the necessity of circumcision, his concern in Galatians is not simply with ceremonial rituals. His message has a far broader reach than that. He is declaring that *any* attempt to relate to God from a law/obedience perspective is insufficient—whether the focus is on the requirements of either the ceremonial or the moral law. A careful examination of the 30-plus places in which the word "law" (Greek *nomos*) occurs in the epistle illustrates this very point. When Paul mentions the "law" in Galatians the context indicates he almost always has a more general definition in mind (Gal. 2:21; 5:3, 4, 23; 6:13). Thus when he talks about the "law" in Galatians, he does not envision a group of ceremonial regulations versus a separate group of moral requirements. Such strict divisions are really more the result of modern attempts of systematization than they are biblical categories. Rather, when he refers to the law that was "added" 430 years after the covenant made with Abraham, he has in mind *all* of the legislation given to Moses at Mount Sinai, both its ceremonial and moral dimensions.

2. Why was it added?

If Paul's use of the law includes the Ten Commandments, how then can he say that it was "added" at Mount Sinai? That is a good question. It is obvious that he knew the Scriptures well enough to have understood that God's law clearly existed before the Lord presented it to the children of Israel in the wilderness. Scripture includes references to the Sabbath in Genesis and Exodus before the promulgation of the Ten Commandments (Gen. 2:1-3; Ex. 16:22-26), and Abraham is said to have kept God's commandments, statutes, and laws (Gen. 26:5). In fact, even the sacrificial system was not entirely new. All the patriarchs before the Exodus offered animal sacrifices. If "added" does not require that the law never existed previously, what then does it mean?

When Paul speaks about the law being "added," he does not imply that it never existed before. Neither does he mean that it was incorporated into God's covenant with Abraham, as if it were a later addendum to a will that somehow altered its original provisions. Rather, the apostle is telling us that the law was "added," or "given," to the children of Israel for an entirely different purpose from that of the promise. It was "added because of transgression."

What purpose does Paul have in mind? We can see a *partial* answer in a similar comment he makes in Romans 5:20: "The law was added so that the trespass might increase" (NIV). The word translated as "added" in the New International Version is a different Greek word than the one the apostle uses in Galatians 3:19. The Greek word in Romans 5:20 is *pareisēlthen* and literally means "came in by a side road." Paul's imagery appears to be this. The main road is the irrevocable covenant that God made with Abraham. The law given at Mount Sinai, however, is a side road. This side road was never intended to be a new way of obtaining God's promises, but a route that could redirect "travelers back to the main road."[5] How does the law do that?

The giving of the law on Mount Sinai stands out as a unique event in salvation history. As *The Seventh-day Adventist Bible Commentary* notes: "The difference between the times before Sinai and those afterward was not a difference as regards the existence of great laws from God, but as regards the explicit revelation of them."[6] God did not need to reveal His law to Abraham with thunder, lightning, and a penalty of death (Ex. 19:10-23). The Israelites, however, were different. They had lost sight of God's greatness and high moral standards, and as a consequence the extent of their own sinfulness.

The presentation of the law on Mount Sinai revealed to the children of Israel the extent of their sinful condition and their need of God's grace, and it does the same for us today. The Lord did not intend the law to be a 10-step program on how to "earn" salvation. On the contrary, it was given, Paul says, "to increase the trespass" (Rom. 5:20), that is, that sin by the commandment might become exceedingly sinful (Rom. 7:13). The moral law with its "Thou shall nots" reveals that sin is not just a part of our natural condition, but also the violation of God's law (Rom. 3:20; 5:13, 20;

7:7, 8, 13). That is why Paul says that where there is no law there is no transgression (Rom. 4:15). And even the ceremonial laws of sacrifices and offerings were expanded on in both number and detail to point to the brokenness of humanity before God and its need of divine forgiveness. As William Hendriksen explains: "The law acts as a magnifying glass. That device does not actually increase the number of dirty spots that defile a garment, but makes them stand out more clearly and reveals many more of them than one is able to see with the naked eye."[7]

While it is certainly useful to consider Paul's similar comments in Romans 5:20 to help make sense of what he says in Galatians 3:19, it is also important to interpret Galatians in its own context and not solely in light of Romans—a letter that Paul likely wrote nearly 10 years later. While similarities between Galatians 3:19 and Romans 5:20 do exist, there are also important differences that should caution us from interpreting the two passages identically. Two of the most significant are the absence of the word "increase" in Galatians 3:19 and the use in Romans of the word "trespass" (Greek *paraptōma*), a term that specifically refers to a deliberate sinful act, instead of "transgression" (Greek *parabasis*) in Galatians, a more generic term for "disobedience." The use of these two terms in Romans limits the role of the law at Mount Sinai to an entirely negative function—it points out sin. Although this is true, the apostle is not nearly as explicit in Galatians.

In Galatians 3:19 Paul simply says the law was added because of transgression. The general nature of his statement does not limit his meaning to the negative aspect of merely pointing out sin. Rather, his terminology is broad enough to understand the "adding" of the law as also a positive response—"because of sin." As Dunn points out, the adding of the law was not entirely negative—it had the positive benefit of providing a remedy for transgression.[8] From this perspective, Paul seems also to envision "that whole dimension of the law so largely lost to sight in modern Christian treatments of Paul—viz. the sacrificial system, whereby transgressions could be dealt with, whereby atonement was provided."[9] In the same way that the children of Israel had forgotten the gravity of sin during their slavery in Egypt, they had also lost sight of the remedy for sin provided in the sacrificial system. God expanded the laws of sacrifices and offerings connected to the sacrificial system at Mount Sinai in order to point more fully to His plan to provide an ultimate atonement for human sinfulness.

Why was the law "added" at Sinai? The answer is twofold: to point out sin and also to direct His people to the remedy for sin found in the sacrificial system associated with the sanctuary.

3. For how long was it added?

This brings us to our final question. What does Paul mean when he says the law was added "until the offspring should come to whom the promise had been made" (Gal. 3:19)?

Many have understood the passage to indicate that the law given at Mount Sinai was only temporary in nature. It entered 430 years after Abraham and ended when Christ came. Now, to a certain extent that statement is correct. It is true that the sacrificial laws presented to Moses were only symbols foretelling the ultimate sacrifice of Christ. Now that Christ, our Passover lamb, has been sacrificed (1 Cor. 5:7), there no longer exists any need for any earthly animal to be sacrificed (Heb. 9; 10). Some Christians, however, also apply this to the moral law of God. They claim that on the cross Christ not only brought the ceremonial laws to an end, but also did away with the moral law.

Although Paul's use of the law in Galatians does include both its ceremonial and moral aspects, it is not accurate to conclude that in Galatians 3:19 he is proclaiming that the moral law has been abolished. Such a conclusion seems faulty for at least two reasons.

First, Paul specifically denies such allegations. In a similar discussion in Romans 3:31 he asks, "Do we then overthrow the law by this faith?" The word translated as "overthrow" in Greek is *katargeō* . He uses it frequently in his letters, and it can be rendered as to "nullify" (Rom. 3:3), to "abolish," (Eph. 2:15), bring "to nothing" (Rom. 6:6), or even to "destroy" (1 Cor. 6:13). Surely if Paul wanted to endorse the idea that the cross terminated the law, this would have been the occasion to say it. But he not only denies that sentiment with an emphatic no—he actually states that his gospel "establishes" the law. Moreover, it also disagrees with what he says about the importance of the law in Romans 4:15. Even Jesus Himself rejected such an idea in Matthew 5:17-19.

A second reason that Paul does not indicate that Calvary abolished the moral law is that the word translated as "until" in Galatians 3:19 "does not imply a time limit for the action mentioned in the sentence."[10] While the word "until" can at times suggest the end of a specific extent of time, it does not always have this kind of temporal sense, as we can see in several different examples from Scripture. In Revelation 2:25 Jesus says, "Only hold fast what you have *until* I come." Does Jesus mean that once He returns we no longer need to be faithful? Certainly not! Or how about Paul's instructions to Timothy? "*Until* I come, devote yourself to the public reading of Scripture, to exhortation, to teaching" (1 Tim. 4:13). While Paul's arrival would certainly alter some things, it does not mean that Timothy would cease doing any of those things. In each example "until" does not imply an end to the activity described. It merely emphasizes a change that occurs.

The same is true in Paul's use of the word "until" in Galatians 3:19. The role of the law did not end with the coming of Christ. It continues to point out sin. What Paul is saying is that the advent of Christ marks a decisive turning point in human history. While the giving of the law on Sinai was the defining point in Israel's history, the incarnation of Christ far outshines it. Christ can do what the moral and ceremonials laws could never accomplish—provide a true remedy for sin, that is, justify sinners and by His Spirit fulfill His law in them (Rom. 8:3, 4). The apostle expands on this concept in greater detail in verses 23-26, and we will continue our discussion of it then.

Living in Light of the Promise Today

Since we are spiritual descendants of Abraham, God's covenantal promises with Abraham is also His promises to us. We have a right to them just as much as Abraham. So whenever the sense of our own failure weighs us down with the hopeless feeling of guilt and condemnation, may we find comfort in remembering that our hope does not rest in *our* obedience to the law, as important as that is, but rather in God's irrevocable *promise* given to Abraham and accepted by faith. Our focus needs to be on Christ and not on our failures or even on "our" achievements. For it is only by concentrating on Christ that we can follow His leading and will for our lives.

---

[1] Donald Guthrie, *Galatians,* New Century Bible Commentary (Grand Rapids: Eerdmans, 1973), p. 101.

[2] *Ibid.*, p. 102. (Italics supplied.)

[3] F. Matera, Galatians, p. 132.

[4] See Woodrow W. Whidden, *E. J. Waggoner: From the Physician of Good News to Agent of Division* (Hagerstown, Md.: Review and Herald, 2008), pp. 98-105.

[5] Timothy George, *Galatians,* The New American Commentary (Nashville: Broadman and Holman, 1994), vol. 30, p. 253.

[6] *The Seventh-day Adventist Bible Commentary* (Washington, D.C.: Review and Herald, 1956, 1980), vol. 6, p. 959.

[7] William Hendriksen, *Exposition of Galatians,* New Testament Commentary (Grand Rapids: Baker, 1979), p. 141.

[8] James D. G. Dunn, *The Epistle to the Galatians,* Black's New Testament Commentary (Peabody, Mass.: Hendrickson, 1993), pp. 189, 190.

[9] *Ibid.*, p. 190.

[10] Erwin Gane, *The Battle for Freedom* (Boise, Idaho: Pacific Press, 1990), p. 79.

CHAPTER 7

The Law as Our *Paidagōgos*

I will never forget her reaction. Her body language left no doubt in my mind what she was thinking. Watching her shake her head back and forth made it clear that she was completely befuddled by Paul's comments in Galatians about the law. I had been in Botswana for several days presenting a number of topics along with two colleagues at a Bible conference for pastors and their wives. The conference theme was Scripture in Theology, Leadership, and Life. It had been a wonderful week of spiritual fellowship and Bible study. As the meetings drew to a finish, one of my colleagues tackled one of the most challenging topics in the New Testament—Paul's view of the law. His particular focal point was Galatians 3:22-25 in which Paul writes, "Now that faith has come, we are no longer under the supervision of the law" (verse 25, NIV). The reaction from the audience indicated that the passage was one in which they were interested in better understanding. But as my colleague began explaining the various nuances of the passage, I could not help noticing the changing reaction of one of the women sitting just a few seats away from me. She was clearly struggling to make sense of Paul's statement. At first she only shifted back and forth in her chair uneasily. But eventually her facial expressions began to change, giving way to a furrowed brow that made it clear she was completely puzzled.

Although it looked to me as if there was little hope for clearing up her initial confusion, a ray of hope brought a momentary reprieve to the disconcerted expressions on her face. The hope came with a statement my colleague made. He said there was a way to make Paul's difficult comments in Galatians simpler to understand. The key was to examine the apostle's use of the identical phrase in 1 Corinthians 9:21-23. While I followed along in my Bible as he read the passage, I was now more interested in seeing if his suggestion would make any change in the woman's reaction—

and it did, just not in the way I expected. As my colleague read, "To those under the law I became as one under the law (though not being myself under the law) that I might win those under the law," the woman began to shake her head back and forth vigorously. And I could see her saying, "I'm not sure that makes it any simpler." I will never forget her reactions, for they will forever be the mental picture I associate with Peter's comments about there being "some things" in Paul's letters "that are hard to understand" (2 Peter 3:16).

So while I hope this chapter will make Paul's comments on the law a little clearer for you, if it does not, just remember that you are neither the first nor the last person to have struggled to comprehend his writing. And although we wade into a potentially difficult passage, be encouraged. Of all the difficult topics in the world that can occupy the human mind, what better subject is there to ponder than the mysteries contained in God's Word? Besides, even a momentary glimpse of the spiritual insights buried in Paul's writings far outweighs the risk of getting stumped in the process of our investigation!

The Relationship of the Promise and the Law

The basic question is this: Is Paul for the law or against it? Is the law a boon or a bane? This one issue has probably vexed and divided Pauline scholars more than any other topic. The difficulty in answering our question lies in the fact that his comments on the law can often seem contradictory. At times he seems to paint a rather disparaging picture of the law, while at other times he can speak positively of the law as being "holy and righteous and good" (Rom. 7:12). Such diverse expressions have led to a legion of varied opinions among scholars, with Paul being "evaluated as almost everything from antinomian through schizophrenic to Pharisee on this issue."[1]

While it might be tempting simply to ignore or to sidestep the topic, we cannot. The law is part and parcel of Paul's message to the Galatians. It plays a fundamental role in how he conceives the nature of the gospel. We can see this in the simple fact that he refers to the law in Galatians and Romans (roughly 75 and 30 times, respectively) more frequently than all of his other letters combined (15 times). And of all the various places in Galatians and Romans in which the law plays a fundamental role in Paul's exposition, no single place affects how one views the relationship between the law and the gospel more than Galatians 3:21-25. The standard understanding of the passage typically sees the law from an entirely *negative* perspective. Many interpret it something like this: "The law was a temporary institution ultimately done away with by Christ's death on Calvary." Such a view implies that Christians no longer need concern themselves with observing the law. What should we make of such a claim?

So far Paul's comments about the law in Galatians have been largely negative. He has made it clear that works of the law justify no one (Gal. 2:16), that God's covenant with Abraham was based not on the law but solely on faith (Gal. 3:15), and that one reason He gave the law on Mount Sinai was to show the Israelites how sinful they were in His sight (verse 19). God's promise to Abraham stands as the defining moment in the history of Israel. And as glorious as the giving of the law was on Mount Sinai, the law does not alter in the least His promise given to Abraham (verse 17). It was a promise that the Lord gave freely with no required prerequisites and only one required element necessary to receive it—faith (verse 18).

Recognizing that his comments might lead the Galatians to mistakenly conclude that he has an entirely disparaging view of the law, Paul asks the next question he knows his opponents are probably wondering. If the law does not alter the promise that God made to Abraham and his descendants, does the law then work against the promise? Is it contrary to the promise? Or does the law offer an alternative means to the same promise? Paul's answer to such questions is an emphatic no!

The idea that the law is somehow in conflict with the gospel was preposterous to him. Not only does he categorically deny such allegations—he gives a simple reason such a conclusion is entirely untenable. The law cannot be "contrary" to the promises of God, because the law and the promise are not rivals. They are both part of God's *one and only plan* to save a world torn apart by sin. The law and the gospel simply play different roles.

It might be helpful if we compare the relationship between the law and the gospel promise to the two different groups of athletes on the roster of an American football team. Every football team has two categories of players: those who play on offense and those on defense. Although they perform two different aspects, they are united as one team with one single goal as their objective—victory. In spite of their common objective, however, the offensive and defensive players have different assignments. The goal of those on offense is to move the ball down the field and to score points. The job of the defense is to stop their opponents from moving the ball and to prevent them from scoring points. For someone to say that the defensive players of a football team are opposed to the offensive players on the same team would be ridiculous, for they work together to achieve the same common objective. To a certain extent, this is similar to the relationship of the law and the promise.

The fact that God never intended that the law would be a legitimate source for securing eternal life does not make it opposed to the promise. It is simply not the role that God has assigned to the law. In fact, Paul uses an interesting Greek sentence structure in Galatians 3:21 to highlight this very point. The technical term for what he employs is a contrary-to-fact conditional sentence. It refers to the way an author can construct a sentence to indicate that he or she is *assuming* an untruth merely for the sake of the argument. Thus the original sense of what Paul says in Galatians 3:21 goes something like this: "If a law had been given that could give life [and of course we know that it is impossible for the law to do that], then righteousness would indeed be by the law."

It is not the law's fault that it cannot give life. God never intended for it to do that. The law can testify to what is right and wrong, but it is unable to forgive sin or give humans the moral power to obey its commands. Of course, this does pose a problem for humanity. Because of the devastating consequences of sin, no descendant of Adam (outside of Jesus) has ever fully obeyed the law. As a result, rather than offering life to sinners, the law becomes a source of condemnation and death—exactly the predicament of the person that Paul describes in Romans 7 who tries to follow God's law in his or her own strength (cf. Rom. 7:10-20).

The Scandalous Teachings of Marcion

So is the law itself evil because it condemns sin and pronounces sinners guilty? Unfortunately, many have assumed exactly that—in fact, it even goes back to the early stages of Christianity and the teachings of an influential individual named Marcion.

According to tradition, Marcion was the son of an early Christian bishop. As a youth he had the privilege of growing up in a Christian home in which he was able to read the stories from the Old Testament and to become acquainted with the books and letters that eventually became known as the New Testament. Of all that he read, Marcion was fascinated most by the letters of the apostle Paul and in particular Paul's message that salvation was by faith apart from the law.

Marcion, however, took the apostle's words to an extreme conclusion, and the results were disastrous. The distinction the apostle makes between the law and the gospel became absolute for Marcion. He reasoned that if gospel is the good news of mercy, love, forgiveness, and deliverance, the law must then be the exact opposite. As such, the law had nothing good associated with it. He viewed it simply as a collection of harsh regulations that result in condemnation, punishment, and death.

But Marcion did not stop there. He imagined the dichotomy between the law and the gospel to reflect the contrast between the Old Testament scriptures and the writings of the New Testament. In contrast to the loving and merciful God in the New Testament, Marcion argued that the God of the Old Testament was harsh, unforgiving, and entirely wrathful. In fact, the whole reason that Jesus came to earth was to save the human race from the wrathful Creator-God of the Old Testament and His strict laws. Thus for Marcion, true Christianity was not the culmination of all the promises and prophecies in the Old Testament. It was a radically new religion that had absolutely no connection to Judaism, its God, or its law.

Although Marcion was branded as a heretic and officially excommunicated around the year 144, his teachings continued to be influential for more than a century—and in some places Marcionism was even a serious rival to the early church. But even though the full-fledged teachings of Marcionism disappeared long ago, many Christians still popularize his views in a modified form—albeit unknowingly. In particular, I am referring to Marcion's belief that the God of the Old Testament is unloving and wrathful, and to his entirely negative picture of the law in relation to Paul's gospel message.

The Problem and Our Ultimate Hope

Unlike Marcion, however, Paul does not vilify the law as something evil. After all, it is God's law. If the apostle had an entirely derogatory view of the law, his letter to the Galatians would have been the place to express it. Significantly, however, Paul does *not,* in Galatians 3:22, say that the "law" confined everything under sin. He says that the "Scripture" did. And here "Scripture" is neither a synonym for the law nor a reference to any one particular verse. The term is much broader. It functions as a substitute for God Himself (cf. Gal. 3:8; Rom. 9:17). We can see this in the nearly identical statement Paul makes in Romans 11:32: "For God has consigned all to disobedience, that he may have mercy on all." In fact, the Greek verb translated by "consigned" (*sygkleiō*) in Romans 11:32 is the same verb used in Galatians 3:22.

Thus the problem, as Paul describes it, is not ultimately the law, but sin. And what is sin? For the apostle, sin is not merely a broken commandment or a bad choice, though it certainly does include all of those things (Rom.

71

3:21-31; cf. 1 John 3:4). No, sin is far more sinister and deadly. Paul personifies it as a ruthless cosmic power or a wicked taskmaster (Rom. 2:17; 6:12-14; 7:13-20) whose power extends not only over "all" (Rom. 3:23) but also over "everything" (a neuter plural in Gal. 3:22) in our world (cf. 1 John 5:19).

Paul's point is that the scriptures testify to the true condition of the world before God. The world lies under the power of sin. The Greek verb he uses (*sygkleiō*) literally means to "lock up on all sides," and it vividly indicates that from a human perspective we have absolutely no possibility of escape,[2] for sin's deadly reach is both pervasive and universal in its scope (Rom. 3:10-18)—no one and no thing lies outside of its dominion, neither Jew nor Greek, neither Israel nor the nations. This is the reality of "the present evil age" that Paul mentioned at the beginning of his epistle (Gal. 1:4).[3] All of Scripture testifies to the extent of the human dilemma, from the story of the Fall in Genesis to the unfaithfulness of Israel described in Malachi.

Why did God confine everything under the power of sin? Notice the two words that begin the final clause of Galatians 3:22: "So that." These two words may be small, but they are significant—and more so than any translation can convey. In Greek they are part of what grammatical scholars classify as a purpose-result clause. A purpose-result clause is a syntactical construction that indicates *both the intention of a given action and its sure accomplishment.*[4] In this case it demonstrates that God's act of confining all under sin had both a purpose and a result behind it—the redemption of sinners. He placed the whole world under the power of sin so that fallen humans might realize that their only hope of freedom is the promised salvation He offers to them in His Son.

The question, then, is What role does the law play in relation to God's act of confining all under sin?

The Structure of Paul's Argument

Now we come to some of the most difficult statements the apostle makes about the law. "Now before faith came, we were held captive under the law, imprisoned until the coming faith would be revealed. So then, the law was our guardian until Christ came, in order that we might be justified by faith. But now that faith has come, we are no longer under a guardian" (Gal. 3:23-25). What exactly is Paul saying about the role of the law? How should we interpret the passage?

The first step toward understanding it is the realization that his comments are not independent remarks, but an intricate part of the overall argument he has been developing in the entire epistle. A close reading of this section of Galatians reveals that he makes use of the preposition "under" a total of five times (verses 22, 23, 25; Gal. 4:2; Gal. 4:3, NIV). Such repetition in Paul's writings is not accidental. It always highlights some significant point he is trying to make. In addition, it is important to note that these five prepositions also divide into a pattern within the three separate units of thought that make up his argument in this section of Galatians: 3:21, 22; 3:23-29; and 4:1-7. The flow of his thought and the repeated use of the preposition suggest that verse 22 stands as the base statement from which the subsequent passages develop and expand. This seems to be confirmed by the fact that each of the final two thought units make use of an analogy to explain the meaning of the prepositional phrase that begins with the word "under."

The following table demonstrates the logical structure of Paul's argument as well as its chiastic form. (In chiastic structures the second part is a mirror image of the first part. The conclusion or point to be made occurs in the center instead of at the end, as in modern Western thought.)

Scripture confined everything **under** sin (**Gal. 3:22—Paul's principal thesis**)
    a. We were guarded **under** the law (**verse 23—our past condition**)
        b. We are no longer **under** a guardian (**verse 25—an analogy**)
            c. You are all sons (**verses 26-29—our present condition**)
        b. We were **under** guardians and managers (**Gal. 4:2—an analogy**)
    a. We were **under** the basic principles (**verse 3, NIV—past fact and present danger**)[5]

Viewed from this perspective, Galatians 3:22 has a dual purpose. It provides an answer to the question that Paul raises in verse 21, and it serves as the base statement from which his argument in Galatians 3:23-4:7 develops. The implications of what it means to be "under sin" leads first to a more detailed explanation of the relationship between the promise and the law, and then to the relationship between heirs and the law. With this larger picture in mind, we now turn our attention to Paul's terminology.

Paul's Terminology

So far he has made three basic points about the law: (1) the law does not nullify or abolish God's promise made to Abraham (Gal. 3:15-20); (2) it was added on Mount Sinai because of transgression, and (3) the law is not opposed to the promise (verses 21, 22). The apostle now turns his attention to what the law does and how the coming of the promised Messiah affects its role. What role does the law actually play? Although Paul said it was added "because of transgressions" in Galatians 3:19, he expands on what he means by that with the use of three significant words used to describe what the law does and what it is like: "kept" (verse 23, KJV), "shut up" (verse 23, KJV), and "schoolmaster" (verse 24, KJV). How should we understand those terms?

For the sake of comparison, observe from the table below how various versions of the Bible have translated the three terms Paul employs in relation to the law in Galatians 3:23, 24: "Now before faith came, we were held captive under the law, imprisoned until the coming faith would be revealed. So then, the law was our guardian until Christ came, in order that we might be justified by faith."

KJV	NJKV	NIV	ESV	NRSV	NASB
kept	kept	held prisoners	held captive	imprisoned	kept in custody
shut up	kept	locked up	imprisoned	guarded	shut up
schoolmaster	tutor	put in charge	guardian	disciplinarian	tutor

As the chart above indicates, many modern Bible translations interpret Paul's comments about the law in Galatians 3:23, 24 in a somewhat negative tone. The original Greek, however, is not nearly so one-sided. The word translated as "kept" (KJV) comes from one that literally means "to keep" or "to guard." Although it can be used in a negative sense as to "hold in subjection" or to "watch over" (see 2 Cor. 11:32), in the New Testament it generally has a more positive sense of "protecting" or "keeping" (cf. Phil. 4:7; 1 Peter 1:5).

The same is true of the word translated as "shut up" (Gal. 3:23, KJV). The word in Greek means "to shut," "to close," or "to enclose," and depending on its context it can have positive, negative, or even neutral connotations. For example, the Septuagint translation of the Old Testament employs it to refer to the act of God in "closing" the wombs of the wives of Abimelech until the ruler returned Sarah to her husband, Abraham (Gen. 20:18). It can also be used of individuals confined to a specific geographical area or in various cities (Ex. 14:3; Joshua 6:1; Jer. 13:19). In the New Testament it can apply to the nets that "enclosed" the miraculous catch of fish by the disciples in Luke 5:6, or the process by which God "confines" or "imprisons" people under sin (Rom. 11:32; Gal. 3:22).

So how does Paul understand the law from the perspective of the two Greek words translated as "kept" and "shut up" in Galatians 3:23? Should we interpret them in a negative, positive, or neutral sense? Because the terms can be approached from so many different viewpoints, we cannot make any final decision until we first determine the role of the law as the *paidagōgos* in verses 24, 25.

The Law as Our *Paidagōgos* (Gal. 3:24, 25)

The idea of the law guarding and confining brings to Paul's mind the role of the *paidagōgos* in Greco-Roman society.[6] The *paidagōgos* was a slave that Roman society placed in a position of authority over the master's son or sons from the time they turned 6 or 7 until they reached maturity. The responsibilities of a *paidagōgos* were so manifold that it is difficult to find a single equivalent word in English that encapsulates them all (as the various translations of the term in the chart above indicate). He was something like a nanny, a chauffeur, a tutor, a nurse, a bodyguard, and a parent all rolled into one. His duties would include taking care of his charge's physical needs, such as drawing his bath, providing him with food and clothes, and caring for him when he was sick. The *paidagōgos* ensured that his master's son went to school and did his homework. In addition, he was not only expected to teach and practice moral virtues, but to make sure also that the child learned and practiced them himself. But of all of the various things a *paidagōgos* might do, his primary task boiled down to protection, prevention, and correction.

A number of interesting descriptions in Greco-Roman literature provide a good illustration of the basic responsibilities of the *paidagōgos*. For example, Libanius, a Greek rhetorician living in the late Roman Empire, vividly describes the protective role of the *paidagōgos*.

"For pedagogues are guards of the blossoming youth, they are keepers, they are a fortified wall; they drive out the undesirable lovers, thrusting them away and keeping them out, not allowing them to fraternize with the boys, they beat off the lover's assaults, becoming like barking dogs to wolves."[7]

His description is of particular interest, since the word "guards" comes from the same root word that Paul uses in Galatians 3:23 to describe the role of the law ("we were guarded under the law"). Another interesting illustration occurs as part of Cain's response when God's asks him about his missing brother Abel. According to the Jewish historian Josephus, Cain retorted "that he was not his brother's guardian [*paidagōgos*] to keep watch over his person and his actions."[8] The protective responsibility of a *paidagōgos* was taken so seriously that at times a *paidagōgos* would even give his life in an attempt to safeguard that of his master's son.

While the master's son certainly valued the protective aspects of a *paidagōgos,* he did not always appreciate the preventive and corrective duties that went along with it—even when they were for his own good. For example, Martial, the legendary Roman poet, complained to his *paidagōgos,* "You ban fun, you bar girls, you won't allow me liberties."[9] Aristides provides an interesting list of the type of admonitions a *paidagōgos* might give: "'It is not proper to stuff yourself full,' and 'walk on the street in a seemly way, and rise for your elders, love your parents, do not be noisy, or play dice, or' (if you wish to add this) 'cross your legs.'"[10] The Roman philosopher Seneca provides a similar collection of chidings: "Walk thus and so; eat thus and so. This is the conduct proper for a man and that for a woman; this for a married man and that for a bachelor."[11] It is no wonder that Philo can confidently say that when the *paidagōgos* "is present his charge will not go amiss."[12]

While some pedagogues were certainly kind and loved by their wards, the dominant description of them in ancient literature is as strict disciplinarians. It was their duty to ensure obedience, whether secured by wise counsel, harsh threats and rebukes, or by whipping and caning if necessary. "As a result, the life of a child under the control of a *paidagōgos* was strictly supervised" and devoid of any real "measure of freedom."[13]

Paul envisions God's law from this same perspective. It is like a *paidagōgos.* In Galatians 3:23 the apostle describes the law as a controlling power (we are under the law) that both "guards" and "condemns." What law is it that both guards and condemns us? Paul's analogy and terminology suggest that limiting the law exclusively to the ceremonial law with its instructions about sacrifices and offerings would fall short of the confining role that he describes. As we saw previously, his view of the law is typically much broader than that. For him, God's law encompasses both its ceremonial and moral aspects. It is God's law as a whole that both guards and confines.

So how should we understand the apostle's comments about the law in Galatians 3:23-25? We have seen that the terminology he uses can by itself be either positive or negative. And what about the role of the *paidagōgos*?

Does Paul envision it as positive or negative? Both questions really involve a much larger and more fundamental issue. Why does the law limit our personal freedom, supervise every aspect of our lives, and condemn us when we fail? The answer is related to Paul's previous statement in Galatians 3:22. God's law was necessary "because we are also held in the custody of sin's prevailing influence. We are, therefore, strapped up, as it were, with the bridle of the Law which makes clear to us our obligation, supervises our conduct, and rebukes and punishes our wrongdoing."[14]

So, again, is the law positive or negative? It is true that the law does have the negative role of pointing out and condemning sin. But it also has the positive function of guarding and protecting us from evil. And even the negative aspect of condemning sin ultimately has the positive objective of helping us realize our need for Christ. Unless the law drives us to Christ by condemning our sin, we would never recognize our need of the forgiveness and deliverance that is in Him. So what is the answer? Perhaps it is not no, or even yes. Instead the best answer is simply to say that the law in all its capacities is simply *necessary*.

Ellen White recognized this fact more than 100 years ago when a number of Adventist ministers were trying to claim that the law in Galatians 3:23-25 had to be exclusively either the ceremonial or moral law. "What law is the schoolmaster to bring us to Christ? I answer: Both the ceremonial and the moral code of ten commandments."[15] She made an additional comment on the same issue some time later that reveals she understood Paul's comments from within the larger perspective of his argument.

"'The law was our schoolmaster to bring us unto Christ, that we might be justified by faith' (Gal. 3:24). In this scripture, the Holy Spirit through the apostle is speaking especially of the moral law. The law reveals sin to us, and causes us to feel our need of Christ and to flee unto Him for pardon and peace by exercising repentance toward God and faith toward our Lord Jesus Christ. . . . The law of ten commandments is not to be looked upon as much from the prohibitory side, as from the mercy side. Its prohibitions are the sure guarantee of happiness in obedience. As received in Christ, it works in us the purity of character that will bring joy to us through eternal ages. To the obedient it is a wall of protection."[16]

The Place of the Law in Salvation History

One final question remains. Although we have argued that the law is certainly necessary in light of the sin problem, how does this correlate with Paul's statement that once "faith has come, we are no longer under a guardian" (Gal. 3:25)? What are we to make of it? We need to understand his comments in Galatians 3:23-25 from two different perspectives—first from that of salvation history, and second from the story of our own experience.

The primary context in which Paul has been developing his argument with the Galatians is on the basis of God's redemptive work in the course of human history. He has already outlined how the Lord revealed Himself to Abraham and presented to him a wonderful promise and how the giving of the law on Mount Sinai 430 years later did not in any way alter that promise. Yet beginning with his first reference to the giving of the law in verse 19, Paul attaches a temporal aspect to it by the use of the word "until." This temporal aspect occurs multiple times within verses 23-25. And in each case, as we will see below, the temporal aspect is always related to the appearance of Jesus, the promised Messiah.

In addition to the historical and temporal aspect, it is important to note also the pronouns Paul uses in Galatians 3:23-29. He begins with "we" (verses 23, 24, 25) and then switches to the plural pronoun "you" (verses 26, 27, 28, 29 [twice]). The "we" refers to the Jewish believers in the Galatian churches. They are the ones acquainted with the law, and Paul has been speaking to them in particular since Galatians 2:15. The "you all" involves the Gentile converts. How does all this fit together?

Paul is contrasting the place of the law before and after Christ, a point he states directly in verse 24: "the law was our guardian until Christ came." And he repeats it in verses 23 and 25, though indirectly by referring to the coming of "the faith." The use of the word "faith" with the definite article "the" in Greek suggests that Paul is not talking merely about a person's personal faith, but about Christ. Immediately before verse 23 the apostle employs the word "faith" in connection with Jesus. In Greek verse 22 literally reads that God's promise is based on the "faith of Jesus." The same expression as Paul used in Galatians 2:16, it can be translated from the Greek as the "faithfulness of Jesus." It is His faithfulness that offers hope to the human condition under sin (Gal. 3:22). So as Paul transitions to verse 23, he is still so captivated by the "faithfulness of Christ" that he refers to Christ as "the faith." He does the exact same thing in verse 25. His terminology indicates that the coming of Christ makes a distinct difference in salvation history.

Unfortunately, many have interpreted Paul's comment as a complete dismissal of the law. But that makes little sense, however, in light of his positive comments about the law elsewhere (e.g., Rom. 3:31; 7:7, 12, 14).

What changed then with the coming of Christ?

God's law did not cease to exist with the arrival of Christ. Sure certain aspects of it were fulfilled, but its moral truths continue to be true today as much as they were 4,000 years ago. What has changed is the position of the law in relation to God's people. It is no longer the ultimate authority that regulates life, for we are called to live a life that is pleasing to Christ (1 Thess. 4:1). Paul refers to this as walking in the Spirit (Gal. 5:18). It does not mean that the moral law is no longer applicable—that was never the issue. Christ, however, transcends the law. He is the epitome of all that it requires and more (Gal. 6:2; 1 Cor. 9:21). We do not merely follow a set of rules—we follow Jesus. And He does what the law could never do—He writes His law on our hearts (Heb. 8:10) and makes it possible for the righteous requirement of the law to be fulfilled in us (Rom. 8:4). Furthermore, we are no longer under the law's condemnation (verse 3). As believers we are in Christ and enjoying the privilege of being under grace (Rom. 6:14-15). And that gives us the liberty of serving Him wholeheartedly without fear of being condemned for mistakes we might make in the process.

Thus the coming of Christ marks a fundamental shift in the scope of salvation history. Yes, we continue to observe the law today, but conformity to the law is not our ultimate goal. The goal of every Christian is ultimately conformity to Christ. For it is in conformity to Christ that we truly encompass all that the law requires. In the life, death, and resurrection of Jesus, the promised Messiah, the law has been overshadowed. Christ first and Christ last—that is the nature of the Christian life.

Although Paul develops his argument in the light of salvation history, we would be amiss if we did not also interpret it in light of our own personal spiritual journey as well. The very fact that he uses the word "the faith" as a reference to Christ (Gal. 3:23) seems to justify the idea of understanding the coming of "faith" as a secondary reference to the dawn of faith in our own lives. Although Christ has come, many of us often live our lives as if He had not. We find ourselves continuing to struggle under sin. In those periods of our lives God's law acts as a *paidagōgos,* hunting us down, declaring our sin, giving us a guilty conscience, and in the process always seeking to drive us to Christ as our only hope. Until the day that the power of sin has not only been conquered but also destroyed arrives, God's law will continue its role of identifying and condemning sin. And personally speaking, I am thankful that it does.

Although Paul's argument is complicated, his point is simple. The law is not at odds with God's promises to Abraham and his descendants. Nor does it offer an alternative way of achieving salvation. On the contrary, although the promise and the law have different roles and functions, they both play an important part in God's overall plan of salvation being worked out in the course of human history—and by spiritual application to our own life experiences as well. Yet in light of all that God has done, the defining moment in the scope of salvation history for us as Christians is not the presentation of the law on Mount Sinai, nor even God's giving of the promises to Abraham. No. It is the one event that has forever changed the course of human history—the incarnation of Christ.

[1] John Fischer, "Paul in His Jewish Context," *The Evangelical Quarterly* 57 (1985): 211.

[2] D. Guthrie, *Galatians,* p. 107.

[3] J. Dunn, *The Epistle to the Galatians,* p. 194.

[4] Daniel Wallace, *Greek Grammar Beyond the Basics* (Grand Rapids: Zondervan, 1996), p. 473.

[5] Linda L. Belleville, "'Under Law': Structural Analysis and the Pauline Concept of Law in Galatians 3:21-4:11," *Journal for the Study of the New Testament* 26 (1986): 54.

[6] *Ibid.*, p. 59.

[7] Libanius *Orations* 58. 7. As quoted in Norman H. Young, "*Paidagōgos:* The Social Setting of a Pauline Metaphor," *Novum Testamentum* 29, no. 2 (1987): 159.

[8] Josephus *Antiquities of the Jews* 1. 56.

[9] Martial, *Epigrams,* trans. James Michie (New York: Modern Library, 2002), p. 143.

[10] Aristides *In Defense of Oratory* 2. 380.

[11] Seneca *Epistles* 94. 8, 9.

[12] Philo *On the Change of Names* 217.

[13] Belleville, p. 60.

[14] *Ibid.*

[15] Ellen G. White, *Selected Messages* (Washington, D.C.: Review and Herald, 1958), book 1, p. 233.

[16] *Ibid.*, pp. 234, 235.

Chapter 8

From Slaves to Heirs

It seems to have been the dream of nearly every child at least once in life—that he or she was not just like every other kid in school, but was actually a prince or a princess. Countless books and movies have capitalized on this childhood fantasy, often with stunning success. As a young boy it was such stories as Little Lord Fauntleroy that caught my imagination and led me to daydream about what it might be like to be a prince. It was no different for my girls when they were growing up—except for them it was Cinderella-like stories that riveted their imagination. Of course, children are not the only ones fascinated with such stories. It seems that the desire to be someone special affects even adults.

In the 1920s people from around the world were mesmerized with the possibility that a woman known as Anna Anderson was not simply a Polish factory worker, but in reality was none other than the Grand Duchess Anastasia of Russia, the youngest daughter of Czar Nicholas II. During the Bolshevik revolution Nicholas II and his entire family were brutally murdered—or so it was thought. Rumors circulated that perhaps his two youngest children had escaped: Anastasia and her brother Alexei. Anderson's claim to be Anastasia caused a media frenzy that lasted for years and spawned several books and movies. The thought that a peasant girl might really be a princess seemed to inspire many with hope for their own troubling situations in life. Thus while Anna had her fair share of opponents, she also had many supporters—some who were even relatives of Nicholas II. Although she was never able to prove her case in court, Anna never once retracted her claim to be Anastasia.

Recent discoveries, however, have proved that Anna was not Anastasia. Not only have DNA tests cast serious doubts on her claim, but Russian forensics specialists have also discovered and verified the graves and bodily remains of the Czar and his entire family. Despite her claims to the contrary, Anna was no princess. She was merely a peasant and a charlatan. In the end her story was nothing more than a fairy tale.

While some might claim that our desire to be something more than we really are is only a childish fantasy, or perhaps a way of escaping from the troubles of real life, I think it is more than that. It is God's whisper to us that our lives are indeed far more valuable than we could ever hope or imagine. This is what Paul urges the Galatians to remember in Galatians 3:26-4:11. Because of what Christ has done, they are now sons and daughters of God, princes and princesses in His kingdom. He encourages them to stop living their lives as if they were slaves, and to enjoy all the rights and privileges that accompany "sonship." Anna Anderson did not need to be a charlatan to be a daughter of a king—she already was. She just never realized it!

Sons of God (Gal. 3:26-29)

The Jewish believers in Galatia had insisted that the Gentiles be circumcised in order to become part of God's covenantal family. As we have seen, their claim led Paul into a lengthy discussion of the role of faith and the law in God's overarching plan of salvation. Starting in Galatians 3:7, Paul pointed out that God's original promise to Abraham and his descendants was based solely on faith. While the law is important, it was not "officially" given to the nation of Israel until some 400 years later. As such, Paul argued, the law was never intended to be God's ultimate revelation. It was to play a transitional role in salvation history something like that of a *paidagōgos*. From a historical perspective (as well as in our own personal experience), the advent of Christ fundamentally changed the way God's followers have related to the law. While it will always point out sin and be an indication of divine will, believers are no longer under its jurisdiction and its condemnation. The Christian will always view the law through the perspective of Christ. And as Christians we are ultimately under the law of Christ (Gal. 6:2; 1 Cor. 9:21).

Galatians 3:26 marks another stage in the apostle's argument. Paul gives a second reason believers are no longer under the law's jurisdiction: they are God's "sons" who have reached the age of maturity. They are no longer minors but adults. Whereas the apostle previously explained the relationship between the law and the promise, he now turns his attention to the relationship between the law and sonship. And as he develops the concept of sonship in Galatians 3:26-4:11, it brings an end to his thoughts about the identity of the true sons of Abraham that he first introduced in Galatians 3:7.

We should not take the apostle's exclusive use of the word "sons" as an affront to the feminine gender. His comments in verse 28 certainly indicate that he includes females in this category. Paul highlights "sons" because he has in the back of his mind the family inheritance that his time and culture passed on to the male offspring.

Although it is easy to overlook, his shift in pronouns in verse 26 is significant. Paul had directed his previous comments to the Jewish believers (the "we" in verses 23-25). Now he addresses all the Gentile believers in Galatia by the use of the second person pronoun "you" (plural in Greek). The statement he makes in verse 26 is revolutionary—he addresses the Gentiles as the "sons of God," a designation that God had used as a special term of affection to refer to the nation of Israel (Ex. 4:22, 23; Deut. 14:1, 2, and Hosea 11:1). By calling uncircumcised Gentiles the "sons of God" Paul was completely casting aside the "us" versus "them" mentality promoted by some Jewish believers. The blessing that was to come upon *all* the families of the earth as part of God's promise to Abraham had now become a reality in Christ.

Unfortunately, additions to a family are not always welcome. When someone joins an already-established family, people can often feel threatened, jealous, or even angry. Several years ago our family experienced a little of this when we decided to adopt a poodle. Our youngest daughter particularly opposed the idea. She had never really felt very comfortable around animals, so the thought of having a dog in the house did not excite her. To make matters worse, the poodle we were thinking about getting had been completely shorn of its hair and was anything but cute. I remember her asking such questions as "Why do we have to get a dog? What right does it have to join our family?" (As you can probably imagine, a little time and hair did wonders. Now our daughter and our poodle are nearly inseparable.)

Paul's willingness to include uncircumcised Gentiles into God's covenantal family seemed threatening to many Jewish believers. What right did Gentiles have to become part of Israel without first becoming Jewish? What right did they have to be called the sons of God? The repeated use of the word "for" in verses 26 and 27 indicates the rationale behind the apostle's declaration. The Gentiles are now part of God's covenantal family for two reasons.

First, as Paul has already mentioned repeatedly in his letter (he wanted to make sure we got his point through our thick skulls), the basis for including Gentiles was not because *they* had done anything to deserve it. It was solely on the basis of what Christ had already done. Christ was faithful (verse 26). And because of His faithfulness, Gentiles now enjoy the special relationship with God that had once been exclusive for Israel!

But how can Christ's faithfulness be conveyed to Gentiles? How do they have access to Christ? Once again his use of the word "for" in verse 27 indicates the close logical development of Paul's reasoning. It is through baptism that believers are united to Christ. Why baptism? "Baptism in the New Testament invariably implies a radical personal commitment involving a decisive no to one's former way of life and an equally emphatic yes to Jesus Christ."[1] In Romans 6 Paul describes baptism symbolically as the uniting of our life with Christ in both His death and resurrection. It is interesting to note, however, that the apostle employs a different metaphor in Galatians. He does not compare our being united with Christ in baptism to our dying with Christ, but with the act of being clothed with Christ. Although Paul's metaphors are different, the conclusion is still the same. Our identity is lost in Christ. In the book of Romans the old self is buried, while in Galatians it is completely enveloped in the robes of Christ's righteousness.

Paul appears to have drawn his terminology of "putting on Christ" from the wonderfully vivid passages in the Old Testament scriptures that talk about God clothing his followers with righteousness and salvation. Isaiah, for example, exclaims: "I will greatly rejoice in the Lord; my soul shall exult in my God, for he has clothed me with the garments of salvation; he has covered me with the robe of righteousness, as a bridegroom decks himself like a priest with a beautiful headdress, and as a bride adorns herself with her jewels" (Isa. 61:10; cf. Job 29:14; Ps 132:9).

The apostle's imagery of putting on Christ reminds me of a saying attributed to Mark Twain, the well-known American author: "Clothes make the man." Certainly clothes do cause a difference. I do not know about you, but I always feel good when I look my best—especially when that means a new suit that has been especially tailored to fit my build. It is strange how the right clothes can prompt us to stand up a little taller and to walk and act with more confidence. While there is certainly more to life in this world than fashion, spiritually speaking Twain's remark is right on target. The Bible uses clothing as a significant metaphor of salvation. It represents a Christ-covered life. The metaphor goes all the way back to the story of the Fall in Genesis in which Adam and Eve's attempt to cover their nakedness was not sufficient. God Himself had to provide them with adequate clothes (Gen. 3:21). As we have seen already, the metaphor continues in the Old Testament prophets (Zech. 3:3, 4). Jesus even builds on it in His parable of the wedding feast, in which a guest refuses to dress appropriately (Matt. 22:1-14). Paul also repeatedly refers in his letters to salvation as an act of "putting on" Christ (Rom. 13:14; Col. 3:9, 10; Eph. 4:22-24; 6:11-17). Even the book of Revelation mentions the importance of having clean robes (Rev. 7:13; 22:14). In an age that seems to be obsessed with physical beauty, the idea of "putting on" Christ is a powerful reminder of the "real" clothes that "make the man."

Our union with Christ symbolized through baptism means that what is true of Christ is also true of us. Since Christ is the "seed" of Abraham, as "joint-heirs with Christ" (Rom. 8:17, KJV) we are also heirs to all the covenantal promises made to Abraham and his descendants (Gal. 3:29). Christ's faithfulness is our faithfulness. His identity is our identity. Here is Paul's second reason that God can include Gentiles in His covenantal family. They can be called the "sons of God" because they have been joined in faith to the one true Son of God, Jesus Christ (Gal. 1:15, 16; 2:20).

All that we have as believers is ultimately rooted in Christ. He is the only hope for the unfaithfulness and failures that plagued the Jewish nation down through the centuries, and for all the vices the Gentile world was known for. Christ is the great equalizer. Whether male or female, slave or free, Jew or Gentile, we all are on equal footing in Him. Such distinctions are irrelevant in Christ. We all equally need to have our less-than-perfect lives covered by the spotless robe of His righteousness.

Coming of Age (Gal. 4:1-3)

Having just compared our relationship to God as sons and heirs, Paul now elaborates on that metaphor by including the theme of inheritance. His terminology envisions a situation in which an owner of a large estate has apparently died, leaving all his property to his oldest son. His son, however, is still a minor. And as is the case with similar situations even today, the father's will stipulates that his son is to be "under" the supervision of guardians and managers until he reaches maturity. Ancient wills from the second century testify to such a practice. They set the age of maturity usually around 20 to 25.[2] Before that time comes, the son is master of his father's estate in title only. As long as he is a minor, he is little more than a slave with his life and possessions controlled and managed by others.

Although Paul's analogy here is similar to that of the *paidagōgos* in Galatians 3:24, it has some distinct differences. Whereas the apostle's primary focus in comparing the law to a *paidagōgos* was to highlight its restrictive nature, his focus in Galatians 4 is on the status of the son as a *minor*. We can clearly see this in the Greek word translated as "child" in verses 1 and 3. Instead of using the typical word for child (*pais*), he employs a word (*nēpios*) that specifically refers to a very young child—a minor. It comes from a Greek verb (*nēpeleō*) meaning "to be without power." Thus for the apostle it is not simply a child, but a minor who has not yet reached the level of maturity needed to care for his own legal affairs. Another difference is that the power of the stewards and managers that he describes is far superior to that of a *paidagōgos*. Not only were the stewards responsible for the upbringing of the master's son—they also had charge of all the financial and administrative affairs until the son was mature enough to assume those duties himself.

How are we to understand Paul's analogy? In verse 3 Paul says, "In the same way we also, when we were children [minors], were enslaved to [the Greek word is "under"] the elementary principles of the world." Before we can go any further, we first have to understand what he means when he refers to "the elementary principles of the world."

Scholars dispute over exactly what the apostle intends by the phrase "elementary principles" (Gal. 4:3, 9). The word in Greek is *stoicheia* and literally means "elements." Some have seen it as a description of the basic substances that compose the universe (cf. 2 Peter 3:10, 12), demonic powers that control this evil age (Col. 2:15), or the rudimentary principles of religious life, that is, the ABCs of religion (Heb. 5:12). Paul's emphasis on humanity's status as "minors" before the coming of Christ (Gal. 4:1-3) suggests he has in mind here the rudimentary principles of religious life. Thus he is saying that the Old Testament period with its laws and sacrifices was merely a gospel primer that outlined the basics of salvation. And as important and instructional as the moral and ceremonials laws were to Israel, they were only shadows of what was to come. God never intended them to take the place of Christ. The "we" would once again refer to the status of Jews in relation to the law before Christ.

The apostle's basic point seems to be that regulating one's life around rules of law instead of Christ is like wanting to go back in time. Although Jews were heirs of God promises, their religious life was, in a certain general sense, a time of spiritual immaturity. They were only dealing with the gospel in type—mere shadows of the heavenly realities that would be manifest only in Christ (Col. 2:17; Heb. 8:5). For the Galatians to turn to a law-based religion experience after Christ had already come was like the adult son in Paul's analogy wanting to be a minor again!

What can we draw for our time from his argument? First, we need to focus on Jesus rather than all the rites and rituals associated with Judaism. That is not to say that we cannot glean beneficial insights from studying the Old Testament. In fact, the Old Testament was the only "Bible" the earliest Christians had. Rather, I am talking about being so caught up in all the details and nuances of the types of the gospel prefigured in the Old Testament that Jesus seems only like an appendix rather than the antitype. Second, we should not look to anyone to tell us what we should or should not do in our Christian walk. I am not talking about seeking spiritual advice or following God's instructions recorded in Scripture, but rather not allowing any human being to control our religious behavior. God wants us to serve Him on the basis of our own initiative as adults in a relationship with Him, not on the basis of the directions and rules imposed on us by others as if we were children.

Christ's Decisive Act in Human History (Gal. 4:4, 5)

Jesus' arrival in our world was not random. Paul says He came in the "fullness of time," the precise time that God had prepared. What "time" was that? From a historical perspective it was known as the *Pax Romana* (the Roman peace), a 200-year period of relative stability and peace across the Roman Empire. Rome's conquest of the Mediterranean world had brought peace, a common language, favorable means of travel, and a common culture that facilitated the rapid spread of the gospel. From a biblical perspective it also marked the time that God had appointed for the coming of the promised Messiah according to the prophecies of Daniel (Dan. 9:24-27).

Thus the entrance of Jesus into human history was no accident. "God sent forth his Son" (Gal. 4:4). In other words, He took the initiative in our salvation. Also implicit in these words is the fundamental Christian belief in Christ's eternal deity (John 1:1-3, 18; Col. 1:15-17; Phil 2:5-9). God did not send a heavenly messenger or a substitute—He came Himself. Although the divine preexistent Son of God, Jesus was also "born of a woman" (Gal. 4:4). While the phrase does imply the virgin birth, it more specifically affirms His genuine humanity (cf. Job 14:1; 15:14; Matt. 11:11). It was necessary for Christ to assume our humanity, because we could not save ourselves. By uniting His sinless divinity with our fallen human nature, Christ legally qualified to be our substitute, Savior, and high priest. The phrase "born under the law" (Gal. 4:4) points in two directions. On the one hand it refers to Jesus' Jewish heritage, but it also includes the fact that He bore our condemnation. He was born under the law, so that He might "redeem those who were under the law" (verse 4).

As we learned previously, the word "redeemed" means to buy back. It refers to the price that someone paid to purchase the freedom of either a hostage or a slave. As this context indicates, redemption implies a negative background—a person is in need of being liberated. From what do we need to be freed? The New Testament presents four things: (1) freedom from the devil and his wiles (Heb. 2:14, 15); (2) freedom from death (1 Cor. 15:56, 57); (3) freedom from the power of sin that enslaves us by nature (Rom. 6:22); and (4) freedom from the condemnation of the law (Rom. 3:23, 24; Gal. 3:13; 4:5).

But the ultimate payoff or benefit of Christ's life, death, and resurrection was not only to redeem us (as wonderful as that is), but also that "we might receive adoption as sons" (Gal. 4:5). That involves far more than just redemption, for in Christ we gain much more than we lost in Adam. Paul's use of "we" here appears not only to refer to the Jewish Christians, but also to all the Gentile believers as well (as the "you" implies in verse 6). Because of what Christ has done, both Jews and Gentiles have the privilege of being God's children—for it is only in Christ that the Lord's promise to Abraham and his descendants finds its ultimate fulfillment.

The Privilege of Adoption (Gal. 4:6, 7)

We often speak about what Christ has accomplished for us as "salvation." While that is true, it is not nearly as vivid and descriptive as Paul's unique use of the word "adoption" (Greek *huiothesia*). Although he is the only New Testament author to employ the word, adoption was a well-known legal procedure in the Greco-Roman world. Several Roman emperors during the apostle's lifetime used adoption as the means of choosing their successor when they had no legal heir. In fact, during the first 200 years of the Roman Empire the only emperors who inherited the throne through birth were Claudius (A.D. 41-54), Titus (A.D. 79-81), and Domitian (A.D. 81-96).

Adoption was a legally binding agreement that guaranteed a number of privileges: (1) the adopted son became the true son of his adoptive father; (2) the father agreed to provide all the necessities of food and clothing; (3) the adopted son could not be repudiated; (4) the adopted son could not be reduced to slavery; (5) the natural parents were never allowed to reclaim the adopted son; (6) and adoption mandated the right of inheritance.[3] If such rights were guaranteed on an earthly level, just imagine how much greater are the privileges we have as the adopted children of God!

Building on his imagery, Paul says that the sign of our adoption is the presence of the Spirit of Jesus in our lives (Gal. 4:6). It proves that we are God's children because the Spirit is not our spirit, but the Spirit of Jesus (Phil. 1:19; 1 Peter 1:11), the one who *is* the Son of God (Gal. 1:16, 17; 2:20).[4] But the apostle does not stop there. He says that there is also "proof" that we are God's children. The evidence that he has in mind is not some kind of spiritual razzle-dazzle such as the ability to perform miracles, speak in tongues, or see visions. No, the proof of it is far more basic and profound than that. It is the *right* we have to call God "Abba" (Gal. 4:6; Rom. 8:15, 16). Jewish children used "Abba" to address their father, somewhat like the word "dad" or "papa" today. While students in Jesus' day would use this term for a beloved teacher, Christ is the first person to have ever addressed God as "Abba" (Mark 14:36). In fact, since "Abba" is Aramaic, not Greek, Paul specifically has in mind the practice and very words of Jesus. Since we have been united with Christ we are God's children, and we have the privilege and right of calling Him "Abba" as well.

Why Turn Back to Slavery? (Gal. 4:8-11)

In Galatians 4:8-11 Paul appeals to the Galatians to live the Christian life like sons and not to return to their former state of slavery. To what were the Gentile believers in Galatia enslaved before coming to Christ? The apostle does not describe the exact nature of their former religious practices, but he clearly has in mind the worship of false gods and idols that result in spiritual slavery. Even though Paul is not more specific, he is likely alluding to the religious cult associated with devotion to the Roman emperor. The worship of the emperor and his family as gods became a popular religion across the Roman Empire, especially in Asia Minor and Galatia during Paul's day. Cities vied for the privilege of dedicating a temple to the emperor and expected people to show their allegiance to Rome by joining in the worship. Much like national holidays today, a city's calendar often revolved around days dedicated to the emperor—for example, his birthday, special occasions during his life, and periodic sacrifices. Paul would have encountered all this during his years of ministry across Asia Minor. In fact, archaeologists have uncovered temples and inscriptions related to the imperial cult in 18 of the places in Asia Minor specifically mentioned in the New Testament, including all the seven churches mentioned in Revelation.[5]

What were the Galatians doing that Paul found so objectionable? Many have interpreted his reference to "days and months and season and years" (Gal. 4:10) as not merely a protest against ceremonial laws, but against the Sabbath as well. Such an interpretation, however, goes beyond the evidence. First, we have no list of Jewish customs identical to his list in Galatians. And if he really wanted to single out the Sabbath and other specific Jewish practices, it is clear from Colossians 2:16 that he could have easily identified them by name. Paul, however, is more ambiguous. Furthermore, if he were prohibiting the practice of Jewish ceremonial laws then his censoring the believers in Galatia would be a direct contradiction to the instruction he gives in Romans 14:5 about not condemning someone for observing them or not. What then does he have in mind?

The context indicates that Paul is drawing a more general parallel between the Gentile's former practices in paganism and their willingness to base their new Christian life around works of law. Paul's terminology likely points to "the packed calendar of the ruler cult [that] dragooned the citizens . . . into observing the days, months, seasons, and years which it laid down for special recognition and celebration."[6] Seen from this perspective, his list is far more generic. He is merely trying to "maximize the similarities between the observances the Galatians have left behind and those they are, or are contemplating, taking up."[7]

Keeping the Right Perspective

The preoccupation with circumcision in Galatia was a clear sign to Paul that the church was losing sight of the real essence of Christianity. The English idiom "actions speak louder than words" was true in Galatia. The behavior of the believers there proclaimed that Christianity was primarily something that *you had to do* rather than *Someone you needed to know*. It was a path that would lead either to a faulty sense of spiritual pride or to spiritual discouragement and ultimate failure. The Gentile believers were in danger of falling back into spiritual slavery, trying to *do* everything just right so they might secure the Master's approval. Paul challenges the Galatians to remember their identity in Christ. Instead of slaves, they are God's sons and daughters, with all the rights and privileges that go along with being an heir. Their situation was similar to the story of a discouraged new convert who came to talk with the well-known Chinese Christian, Watchman Nee.

"'No matter how much I pray, no matter how hard I try, I simply cannot seem to be faithful to my Lord. I think I'm losing my salvation.' Nee said, 'Do you see this dog here? He is my dog. He is house-trained; he never makes a mess; he is obedient; he is a pure delight to me. Out in the kitchen I have a son, a baby son. He makes a mess, he throws his food around, he fouls his clothes, he is a total mess. But who is going to inherit my kingdom? Not my dog; my son is my heir. You are Jesus Christ's heir because it is for you that He died.'"[8]

We too are God's heirs, not because of our own merit, but by means of His grace. In Christ we have much more than we ever had before Adam's sin. Let us not forget that in Christ we are sons and daughters of God.

---

[1] T. George, *Galatians,* p. 276.

[2] Belleville, "Under Law," p. 62.

[3] D. R. Moore-Crispin, "Galatians 4:1-9: The Use and Abuse of Parallels," *EQ: The Evangelical Quarterly* 60 (1989): 216.

[4] J. Dunn, *The Epistle to the Galatians,* p. 220.

[5] Hans-Josef Klauck, *The Religious Context of Early Christianity* (Minneapolis: Fortress Press, 2003), pp. 319-325.

[6] Stephen Mitchel, *Anatolia: Land, Men and Gods in Asia Minor* (Oxford: Clarendon Press, 1993), p. 10.

[7] Ben Witherington, *Grace in Galatia* (Grand Rapids: Eerdmans, 1998), p. 299.

[8] Lou Nicholes, *Hebrews: Patterns for Living* (Xulon Press, 2004), p. 31.

CHAPTER 9

Paul's Pastoral Appeal

Mr. Brown was known as a tough, no-nonsense principal who ran his public high school as if it were a state penitentiary. He regularly paced the halls as if he were a guard on the lookout for any trouble from the inmates. It was not all show, either. He had a legendary paddle in his office (with holes drilled throughout it to enhance its effectiveness) that he was not afraid to use if necessary. I had had my fair share of run-ins with school principals before, and I knew that staying clear of Mr. Brown was a good idea.

It was my senior year in high school, and because my family had moved around, it was also my third high school in three years. My life had been out of control for years. I had no interest in spiritual things, and it was clearly manifest in the course my life was taking. When I was a sophomore, I had been arrested for underage drinking and driving, expelled from school for fighting, and even had one of my teachers claim that I was the worst kid in the school. Countless times someone had lectured me about how bad my behavior was, and how I needed to shape up or else.

So when Mr. Brown said he wanted to talk with me, I was prepared for the worst. It was a Friday night. My friends and I had been out drinking. We decided to swing by the high school football game to see if we could find some action—but all we found was Mr. Brown. Or to be more precise, he "found" us.

As he pulled me aside, I expected him to really let me have it. I was prepared for the worst. My defenses were up. After all, I had heard it all before. But to my surprise, he put his arm around me and said, "Carl, what are you doing? Why are you hanging out with those guys? I know you are really a lot better than this." It completely took me off guard, though I didn't let him know it. I said I had no idea what he was talking about and walked away. In reality, however, his approach and words made a deep and lasting impression on me. They marked the beginning of a turning point in my life that along with several other events would lead to my baptism in the summer of my senior year. In that moment I realized that Mr. Brown was different. I felt that he actually cared about me—that I actually mattered.

Something similar happens in Paul's epistle in Galatians 4:12-20. Up until this point in his letter, he has been listing all the theological reasons the Galatians were going down the wrong path. His argument has been detailed and complex, and at times fiery passion has marked his tone (Gal. 1:6-9). But then all of a sudden he stops, breaking off his train of thought and speaking in a markedly different manner to the Galatians. His tone is gentler as he appeals to them from his heart. No doubt his sudden change caught the Galatians off guard, just as Mr. Brown's compassionate appeal did with me.

The Heart of Paul (Gal. 4:12-20)

When many people think about the apostle Paul, they often remember his rougher side—his sharp tongue (Gal. 5:12), his impatience (Acts 15:37-39), and his no-nonsense approach to telling people the truth (Gal. 2:11-14). But that is not the whole picture. He also had a softer side. We see it here. Galatians 4:12-20 is one of the most immensely personal, intimate, and gripping passages in all of his letters. In these verses he, as the well-known English idiom says, "wears his heart on his sleeve." Holding nothing back, he expresses his heartfelt emotions freely and openly, for all the Galatians to see.

The initial indication of the concern that weighs heavily on Paul's heart appears in his personal appeal in verse 12. His "I entreat you" immediately precedes his insistence that the Galatians "become as I am." Unfortunately, some translations do not fully convey the significance of the word he uses. The word is *deomai*. And although it can be rendered as "to urge" (NKJV) or "to entreat" (ESV), the Greek word has a stronger sense of desperation connected to it. For example, one word in 2 Corinthians 5:20 gets translated as "implore" (ESV), "plead" (NLT), or even as "beg" (NASB). So the sense of what he is really saying is "I'm pleading and begging that you change your course!"

Paul's concern was not simply about theological ideas and doctrinal points of view. His heart was bound up with the lives of the people brought to Christ through his ministry. He considered himself more than just a friend—he was their spiritual father, and they were his children (1 Cor. 4:14, 15; 1 Thess. 2:7; Philemon 10). But even more than that, his personal appeal manifests itself in how he compares his concern for the Galatians to the worry and anguish that accompanies a mother in childbirth (Gal. 4:19). The apostle had thought that his previous "labor" had been sufficient for their "safe delivery" when he had founded the Galatian church. But now that the Galatians had wandered from the truth, he was experiencing those labor pains all over "again" to secure their well-being. This was no game for Paul. He knew that their picture of Christ and understanding of what He required of them would affect every aspect of their life—and that even their eternal destiny was ultimately at stake.

Having first described the Galatians as being formed in the womb, Paul mixes his metaphors as he also speaks of them as if they were also expectant mothers themselves. "My little children, for whom I am again in the anguish of childbirth until Christ is *formed* in you!" (verse 19). The Greek word translated as "formed" was used medically to refer to the development of an embryo in a mother's womb.[1] Through his metaphor Paul describes what it means to be Christian—both individually and collectively as a church. To be a follower of Christ is more than just the profession of faith—it also involves a radical transformation into the likeness of Christ. The fundamental issue, as Paul saw it, was far more than about one outward act such as circumcision. For as Leon Morris notes, Paul was "not looking for a few minor alterations in the Galatians but for such a transformation that to see them would be to see Christ."[2]

Now with this basic overview of the passage in mind, let's look a little closer at some of the specific details we find in it.

The Challenge to Become (Gal. 4:12)

One surprising aspect of this section of Galatians is Paul's appeal that the Galatians "become as I am" (Gal. 4:12). His call to "imitation" certainly does not sound very modest. What should we make of his statement?

Several times throughout his letters, he encourages Christians to model his behavior. In each situation he presents himself as an authoritative example that believers should follow. For example, in 2 Thessalonians 3:7-9 he offers himself as an illustration of how the believers in Thessalonica should work to earn their own living and not be a burden on others. He urges the Corinthians to be like him in placing the welfare of others before their own (1 Cor. 11:1). And in Philippians 3:17 Paul encourages believers to share his determination to be faithful to Christ to the very end. While he can call on his followers to emulate his behavior, his concern in Galatians appears to be somewhat different.

Galatians 4:12 does not use the Greek word for "imitate," but instead Paul uses the verb "to be." Why the difference? The trouble in Galatia was not unethical behavior or an ungodly lifestyle, as in the church in Corinth (1 Cor. 5; 6). The issue in Galatia was rooted in the essence of Christianity itself. It was about "being," not "behavior." The apostle was not simply saying, "Act like me," but "Be what I am." The exact same terminology in Galatians 4:12 occurs in his appeal to Herod Agrippa II in Acts 26:29, in which Paul says, "I would to God that not only you but also all who hear me this day might become such as I am—except for these chains." In other words, he is referring to his experience as a Christian whose foundation rests on Christ alone. The Galatians, in contrast, were placing greater value on their behavior than on their identity in Christ.

Although Paul does not specifically say how he wants the Galatians to become like him, the context of the situation indicates that it was not a blanket statement that covered every aspect and detail of his life. Since his concern is with the law-centered religion of the Galatians, the apostle surely has in mind the wonderful love, joy, freedom, and certainty of salvation he had found in Jesus Christ. In light of the surpassing wonder of Christ, Paul had learned to count everything else as rubbish (Phil. 3:8, 9). And he longed that the Galatians themselves would have that same experience.

Of course, whether he is talking about modeling his "behavior" or his "being," it still does not excuse him from a charge of being prideful. While his appeal for imitation may initially surprise us today, I do not believe it is inconsistent with Christian humility. We must understand his statements within their context. First, they do not suggest in the least that he was trying to take the place of Christ. He himself openly acknowledges that the ultimate example for every Christian is Christ and Christ alone (Phil. 2:5-8). In addition, Paul never claimed that he had reached some kind of sinless perfection (1 Tim. 1:15; Phil. 3:12-15). Like all of us, he certainly had things in his life that he wished he could have done over.

Rather than being immodest, Richard Hays believes that the apostle's challenge to his readers about imitation reflects wisdom on his part as a spiritual leader. Why? Because "we learn who we are and how to act only by the example of others. . . . Believing that his own life was in fact conformed to the self-sacrificial example of Christ, Paul was willing to offer himself as a role model."[3] Paul clearly believed that there should be no disconnect between what Christians profess and the lifestyle choices they make on a daily basis. Would that there were more faithful examples among church leaders today. Perhaps our surprise at Paul's comments about imitation says something more about the problems we have become accustomed to seeing in our culture and in our own lives than it does about him.

I Have Become as You Are (Gal. 4:12)

At first glance Paul's statement in Galatians 4:12 makes little sense. How can he appeal to the Galatians to "become as I am" when he says, "I also have become as you are"? If he has become like them, then does not that completely undermine his appeal for them to become like himself? What exactly does he mean?

As we have already seen, he wanted the Galatians to become like him in terms of his faith and confidence in the all-sufficiency of Christ for salvation. His comments about having become like them were a reminder of how, although he was a Jew, he had become a Gentile like them "without the law" so that he might reach them with the gospel—something completely contrary to the way Peter had behaved in Antioch. Peter was choosing to live like a Gentile, but forcing the Gentiles to live like Jews (Gal. 2:14). But instead of distancing himself from Gentiles out of concern for ritual purity (cf. Acts 10:28), Paul freely associated with them as if he were a Gentile himself. The apostle had also learned how to preach the gospel to both Jews and Gentiles—and according to 1 Corinthians 9:19-23, though his gospel remained the same, his method varied depending on the people he sought to reach. "Paul was a pioneer in what today we call contextualization, the need to communicate the gospel in such a way that it speaks to the total context of the people to whom it is addressed."[4]

Some regarded with suspicion his willingness to become like a Gentile in order to reach Gentiles. It seemed dangerous—in fact, it continues to make some people just as uncomfortable today as it did nearly 2,000 years ago. Just how far should one go in trying to contextualize the gospel? And are there ever any limits? Can a person actually wander too far in trying to reach someone for Christ?

Paul's own comments in 1 Corinthians 9:21 indicate that he believed there are indeed limits when it comes to contextualizing the gospel. He mentions, for example, that while one is free to reach out in different ways to Jews and Gentiles, that freedom does not include the right to live a completely lawless lifestyle, for Christians are under the "law of Christ." One author has suggested the following basic guideline: "Insofar as we are able to separate the heart of the gospel from its cultural cocoon, to contextualize the message of Christ without compromising its content, we too should become imitators of Paul."[5]

Although Paul does not provide any specific guidelines for how to contextualize the gospel, Scripture does record several examples of how he sought to do so himself. The most well known example is his attempt to share the gospel with the Epicurean and Stoic philosophers on the Areopagus in Athens (Acts 17:16-34).

In the book of Acts the Gentiles that he typically brings to Christ are pagans who already have an interest in Judaism and have even been attending synagogue. Thus when the apostle shares the gospel with these Gentiles (and Jews), his appeal is that Jesus is the promised Messiah as foretold in the Scriptures (Acts 17:2, 3; 13:17-48).

But in Athens the situation was quite different. Paul attempted to preach the gospel to pagans who did not already have a connection to Judaism and who certainly did not place any value on the Jewish Scriptures. Thus instead of appealing to Scripture, he used an anonymous altar dedicated to an unknown deity and passages from two pagan poets as his connecting points with the Athenians. He proclaimed that the one true God is the Creator of the universe, the sustainer of life, the ruler of all the nations, the Father of human beings, and the judge of the whole world.[6] But when he began to refer to Jesus and His resurrection from the grave, the Athenian philosophers lost all patience and began to mock the apostle.

Often we hear the claim that Paul's method of preaching in Athens was not only unsuccessful but a mistake. Discouraged by the limited number of converts, he allegedly renounced his attempt at contextualizing the gospel and resolved only to preach "Jesus Christ and him crucified" (1 Cor. 2:2). I don't agree. When visiting Athens recently, I had an interesting conversation with a local Greek Christian about whether the apostle's work in Athens was successful. Her response made a lot of sense to me. "I'm not sure why people think Paul's attempt to preach the gospel in Athens was so unsuccessful," she said. "Sure, the book of Acts does not say much about the church in Athens. But it does say that he won at least a handful of converts—and it even names two of them. The fact remains that I am a Greek Christian today because of the message Paul preached 2,000 years ago. How can anyone call that unsuccessful?"

Although he reached out to the Athenians in a nontraditional way, the basic content of his message remained the same. He donned the trappings of another culture in order to share with them a very different worldview than their own. As such, he was willing to live as someone "outside the law" in order to reach those "outside the law" for Christ. We find other examples of this in 1 Corinthians 8:8-13 and Galatians 2:11-14.

G-4

At the same time, Paul was not a slave to his own freedom. In order to help mend relations with Jewish believers who felt he was completely undermining the rich heritage of Judaism, he participated in a purification rite connected with the Jewish Temple. At James' request he even paid the expenses of four Jewish Christians who had taken a Nazirite vow (Acts 21:23-26). Of course, for Paul the whole idea about purification was a nonessential. Since he had been purified in Christ, the apostle could have argued with James that such an act was ridiculous. Free in Christ, he did not need to submit to the Jewish ritual to be purified. Nevertheless, Paul consented. He was willing to live as someone "under the law" if that could make his witness for Christ more effective.

All this raises a basic question for us today. Are we as Christians attempting to contextualize the gospel to the changing world around us? Or have we become so comfortable with the way we have always done evangelism that we are unwilling to try something different? No matter where one stands on the issue of contextualizing the gospel, Paul is clear. One method of reaching out to the community or one set of evangelistic sermons and PowerPoints will not reach everyone for Christ. There needs to be more than one way to share Him.

Then and Now (Gal. 4:13-15)

As Paul pours out his heart to the Galatian believers, he reminds them that their relationship had not always been as difficult and frigid as it had become. Like a spouse reminiscing about the past, he reflects back to the time when he first preached the gospel in Galatia. His relationship with the Galatians had started off so well. What had happened?

Some comments that Paul makes suggest that it had apparently not been his original intention to preach the gospel in Galatia. Some sort of illness had overtaken him on his journey through the region, forcing him either to stay longer in Galatia than expected or compelling him to travel to Galatia for his recovery. What was the exact nature of his malady? Unfortunately, he does not give us all the details that we would like to know. Some have suggested that he contracted a case of malaria, others wonder if he suffered from epilepsy, and still others, on the basis of his reference to the Galatians' willingness to pluck out their eyes and give them to him, propose an eye disease. His illness may also be connected to the "thorn in the flesh" he mentions in 2 Corinthians 12:7-9.

Whatever Paul suffered from, he does tell us that it was so unpleasant that it was a trial not just for him but also even for the Galatians. In a world in which people often saw illness as a sign of divine displeasure (cf. John 9:1, 2; Luke 13:1-4), the apostle's condition could have easily provided the Galatians with an excuse to reject both him and his message. But they did not. Instead, they welcomed him wholeheartedly. Why? There was only one reason. The good news of what Jesus had done for them on Calvary (Gal. 3:1) and the conviction of the Holy Spirit had warmed their hearts. Paul and the Galatians had formed a special bond of affection. They had cared for his physical needs, and he for their spiritual ones. They were so full of thankfulness and love for him that they would have done anything for him—even if it meant their own personal loss (Gal. 4:15). It had been the best of times. Paul's feelings for them had not changed. What reason could they give now for their change of attitude?

Speaking the Truth (Gal. 4:16)

All that Paul had done was to tell the Galatians the truth about their spiritual situation. The expression "speaking the truth" often has the negative connotation of a hard-hitting, no-holds-barred, spare-no-enemies tactic of telling someone the facts, no matter how unpleasant or unwanted they may be. It is like forcing someone to take his or her medicine. You might not like it, but it is for your own good! And if it were not for Paul's comments in Galatians 4:12-20 and a few others scattered throughout his letter (see Gal. 6:9, 10), one might mistakenly conclude that his interest in the truth of the gospel outweighed any expression of love. But that is clearly not the case. If truth and love are genuine, the two can never be separate.

Paul uses the word "truth" three other times in his epistle to the Galatians. He refers to the "truth of the gospel" in Galatians 2:5 and 14. In Galatians 5:7 he asks who hindered them from obeying the truth. Thus for Paul speaking the truth to the Galatians does not involve chastising them for their mistakes, but rather proclaiming to them the wonderful reality of the gospel. Of course it does not mean that the truth never hurts. It does. In fact, it often comes as an offense to human pride. The gospel message of Christ and Christ alone leaves no room for human pride or for boasting in our accomplishments.

And that is exactly Paul's point. In contrast to the candor of his gospel, his opponents were actively courting the favor of the Galatians from selfish motives, not because they loved them. All they really cared about was circumcision. John Phillips nicely summarizes the stark difference between Paul and his opponents. The apostle "had come to evangelize; they had come to proselytize. Paul had come to win them to a Person; they had come to join them to a party. The Galatians would be a star in Paul's crown, no doubt about that. All that the Judaizers wanted, however, was to make them a feather in their cap."[7]

It is unclear exactly what Paul means when he says that his opponents "want to shut you out" (Gal. 4:17). While it may refer to an attempt to exclude them from the fellowship and the companionship of Gentile Christians, it more likely indicates an attempt to deprive the latter of the privileges of the gospel until they "first" submit to circumcision (Acts. 15:1). In either case, the outcome would be the same—the Galatians would then turn to the Judaizers for guidance and spiritual direction. His opponents were looking for a following. The apostle, in contrast, wanted the Galatians to follow Christ.

Wisdom for the Wise

When compared with all the theological doctrines and insights Paul has packed elsewhere in Galatians, we might be tempted to think that Galatians 4:12-20 is not that impressive or significant. It says little, if anything, for example, about the cardinal doctrines that form the theological foundation of the Christian faith. Such an assessment about the relative value of the passage would be completely amiss, however. While it might not say much about church doctrine, it does reveal much about the context in which we should study doctrine and apply it to the every day life of the believer and the church.

First, it should remind us that no matter how important "truth" is to us, the truth is ultimately about God's love for people and not merely a set of nicely packaged beliefs. What good are beliefs if we fail to demonstrate to others that we really care about them personally? We should be interested in them for who they are, not merely in what we want them to do. Second, in a world in which mass production seems like the key to global success, Paul's comments on becoming like others should remind us that we should never look to one method or strategy to reach the world for Christ—no matter how "good" it might appear to be. And finally, though Christ is our ultimate example of the life that we are called to live, as His followers our lives should also be an illustration to others of what it means to be called a Christian.

---

[1] Philo *Special Laws* 3. 117.
[2] Leon Morris, *Galatians: Paul's Charter of Christian Freedom* (Downers Grove, Ill.:

InterVarsity Press, 1996), p. 142.

[3] Richard B. Hays, *First Corinthians,* Interpretation, a Bible Commentary for Teaching and Preaching (Louisville: John Knox Press, 1997), p. 180.

[4] T. George, *Galatians,* p. 321.

[5] *Ibid.*, pp. 321, 322.

[6] John Stott, *The Spirit, the Church, and the World: The Message of Acts* (Downers Grove, Ill.: InterVarsity Press, 1990), pp. 284-288.

[7] John Phillips, *Exploring Galatians* (Grand Rapids: Kregel, 2004), p. 129.

CHAPTER 10

The Two Covenants

Probably no theme in Scripture produces more misunderstanding today than that of the two covenants. Both the New and the Old Testament speak about a "new" and an "old" covenant. And in every case, Scripture describes the new in positive terms while depicting the old as faulty and inadequate. The confusion arises from several negative statements that Paul makes about the law and the old covenant (2 Cor. 3:6-9), and in particular Galatians 4:24, in which he associates the old covenant with the giving of the law on Mount Sinai. As a result, some Christians believe that the giving of the law on Sinai is inconsistent with the gospel. Some have even gone so far as to conclude that the covenant given on Sinai represents a time in human history when salvation rested on obedience to the law. And since that method ultimately proved unsuccessful, God had to usher in a new dispensation in which salvation had its basis no longer in obedience, but rather on grace available through Jesus in the new covenant. Thus many identify Jesus and the New Testament as the new covenant and view the law and the Old Testament as belonging to the old covenant. The problem with this perspective is that it overlooks the fact that Scripture never restricts the new covenant promise to people living after the time of Jesus—it was also a promise given to Old Testament believers long before Jesus' birth. The following chart illustrates the typical dispensational view of the covenants.

Old Covenant = Age Before Calvary	New Covenant = Age After Calvary

Other Christians who have rejected the dispensational interpretation have also puzzled over the two covenants. While they have not made the mistake of identifying the old and new covenants as two different ways of salvation available at different times in history, they have struggled to come to grips with Paul's association of the old covenant with the law given on Mount Sinai. Having traditionally not seen the law as something negative, Seventh-day Adventists, for example, have argued that it not only plays an important role in the life of the believer, but also has a central place in the conflict between Christ and Satan. If the law is not evil, but "holy and righteous and good" (Rom. 7:12), what then are we to make of Paul's connection of it with the old covenant in Galatians 4:21-31? And in what sense is the new covenant superior to the old? To answer such questions, we will first need to examine what a covenant entailed in the Old Testament, and specifically the nature of the covenant that God made with Abraham.

Covenant Basics

The Hebrew word translated as "covenant" is *berît*. Occurring nearly 300 times in the Old Testament, it refers to a legally binding contract, agreement, or treaty that stipulates the nature of a relationship between various individuals. Covenants can involve either mutual agreements by two or more individuals, as in a business contract, or they can be a unilateral decision, like a will. In either case, a covenant required that all the participants would be "faithful" in honoring the obligations associated with their commitment. Types of covenants specifically mentioned in the Old Testament range from personal ones between individuals (Gen. 21:22-34; 31:44-54; 2 Sam. 3:12, 13); marriage contacts (Mal. 2:14); covenants between kings and their subjects (2 Sam. 5:3; 2 Kings 11:17; Jer. 34:8); and alliances between nations (1 Kings 15:19; Eze. 17:13).

While specific details changed from one covenant to another, the heart of every covenant involved a relational aspect that brought with it an obligation of faithfulness by the parties represented. We see a good example of this in the covenant between David and Jonathan. The formal covenant they chose to make with each other comprised much more than just warm feelings between close friends (1 Sam. 18:3). It also "bound them to demonstrate mutual loyalty and loving-kindness in certain tangible ways"[1] to each other. How it worked out in reality we find vividly depicted in the way that Jonathan risked his own safety by speaking favorably in David's behalf when his father, King Saul, was determined to malign David's character. It also appears in how he warned David to flee when Saul had determined to kill him (1 Sam. 19; 20). Jonathan was willing to be faithful to his word, even if it cost him his life.

In the same way that contracts and legal agreements play a part in our contemporary life, covenants had an integral role in defining the nature of everyday relationships between people and nations across the ancient world for thousands of years. One primary difference did exist, however, between now and back then. Whereas we formalize an official agreement by signing our name to a written agreement, in antiquity covenants in the Near East often involved the slaughter of animals as part of the process of making, or literally "cutting," a covenant.

Why the slaughter of an animal? The killing of animals symbolized what would happen to any of the parties if they failed to keep their covenant promises and obligations. An example of this aspect of an ancient covenant appears in the following fragment from a covenant between the Assyrian ruler Ashurnirari V and his vassal Mati'-ilu.

"This head is not the head of a spring lamb, it is the head of Mati'-ilu, it is the head of his sons, his magnates and the people of [his la]nd. If Mati'-ilu [should sin] against this treaty, so may, just as the head of this spring lamb is c[ut] off, and its knuckle placed in its mouth, [...] the head of Mati'-ilu be cut off, and his sons [and magnates] be th[rown] into [...]."[2]

And to think that we complain about all the wasted trees involved in the paper we consume today. That certainly pales in comparison to the number of animals slaughtered as part of ancient agreements. Can you imagine the uproar from animal rights activists if the practice were still common today?

God's Covenant

In addition to the covenants made between humans, one of the most amazing aspects of the Old Testament is that God chose to bind Himself to His people by entering into a formal covenant relationship with them. In fact, the theme of God's covenant with His people is not simply an isolated aspect of Scripture. The dominant image of salvation in the entire Old Testament, it is the definitive way in which God explains His plan to undo the consequences of sin and to restore the human race into a right relationship with Him. As Hans LaRondelle points out: "From Adam to Jesus, God dealt with humanity by means of a series of covenant promises that centered on a coming Redeemer and which culminated in the Davidic covenant (Gen. 12:2, 3; 2 Sam. 7:12-17; Isa. 11). To Israel in Babylonian captivity God promised a more effective 'new covenant' (Jer.

31:31-34) in connection with the coming of the Davidic Messiah (Eze. 36:26-28; 37:22-28)."[3]

Like human covenants, the one that God has made with the human race involved both relationship and obligation. God wants to be our God and for us to relate to Him as His special people. He promises to be faithful to us and asks that we be faithful to Him in return.

The first explicit mention of covenant in Scripture is the one that God originated with Noah. This covenant really comes as a surprise, since it follows on the heels of universal corruption, violence, and faithlessness toward Him (Gen. 6:5, 6). Nevertheless, the Lord promises to Noah, "I will establish my covenant with you, and you shall come into the ark, you, your sons, your wife, and your sons' wives with you" (verse 18). The word translated as "establish" (Hebrew *heqim*) does not indicate the beginning of a new covenant, but the "'maintaining' of a commitment to which God had pledged Himself earlier, implying that God had previously made a covenant with human beings."[4] And what previous covenant does this refer to? It points back to God's promise of redemption given to Adam and Eve in Genesis 3:15—the promise that God would one day undo the divine curse that had come upon the world as a result of sin.

What in particular was the nature of God's covenant with Noah? It was a universal one made with not only the entire human race but also all living creatures (Gen. 9:8-10). And what is so striking about it is that the Lord does all the promising—He requires nothing in return. The rainbow is His promise that a flood will never again destroy the earth (verse 11). An example of God's grace, the rainbow perpetually reminds us that He is trustworthy. He will always be faithful to His covenant promise.

The Abrahamic Covenant (Gen. 15)

God's initial promises to Abram in Genesis 12:1-3 are some of the more powerful passages in the Hebrew Scriptures. "Go from your country and your kindred and your father's house to the land that I will show you. And I will make of you a great nation, and I will bless you and make your name great, so that you will be a blessing. I will bless those who bless you, and him who dishonors you I will curse, and in you all the families of the earth shall be blessed."

The passage is all about God's grace. It is God who takes the initiative, and it is God, not Abram, who makes the promises. Abram had done nothing to earn or merit divine favor, nor is there any indication that suggests that God and Abram had somehow worked together to come up with the agreement. The Lord does all the promising and does not ask Abram to promise anything in return. Instead, He calls upon the patriarch to have faith in the surety of His promise, and not some flimsy type of so-called faith. Abram is to stake his life on that faith by leaving his extended family at the age of 75 and heading to the land that God promised.

God's promises to Abram were not an isolated event. They were simply another stage in His great plan to save the world. "With the 'blessing' pronounced on Abram and through him on all human beings, the Creator renewed His redemptive purpose. He had 'blessed' Adam and Eve in Paradise (Gen. 1:28; 5:2) and then 'blessed Noah and his sons' after the flood (9:1). This way God clarified His earlier promise of a Redeemer who will redeem humanity, destroy evil, and restore Paradise (Gen. 3:15). God confirmed His promise to bless 'all peoples' in His universal outreach."[5]

While Abram responded in faith to God's word, the child implied in the divine promise never arrived. Finally, after 10 years of waiting for the promised son to be born, the patriarch began to wonder if he had somehow misunderstood God's intentions. Did the Lord want him to legally adopt his trusted servant Eliezer as his son? The divine response was clear. Abram would not only father his own son, but his descendants would be as innumerable as the stars. Scripture then records one of the apostle Paul's favorite passages: "And he believed the Lord, and he counted it to him as righteousness" (Gen. 15:6).

Unfortunately, most people end the story of Abram in Genesis 15 with verse 6. When we fail to note "the rest of the story," as the famous American radio broadcaster Paul Harvey used to say, we end up not only creating a false picture of the patriarch, but also missing out on one of the most meaningful experiences in his life. Let me explain.

On the basis of passages such as Genesis 15:6, it is easy to glorify Abram as a man of faith who never had any questions or doubts. Scripture, however, paints a different picture. Abram believed, but he also had questions along the way. When God renews His promise to him in Genesis 15:7, Abram actually asks God for a little more proof. "O Lord God, how am I to know that I shall possess it?" (verse 8). Like the father in Mark 9:24, Abram basically says to God, "I believe; help my unbelief." In response, the Lord graciously assures Abram of the certainty of His promise by formally entering into a covenant with him.

What makes this passage so surprising is not the fact that God establishes a covenant with Abram, but the extent to which God was willing to condescend to do so. Unlike other rulers in the ancient Near East who shirked at the idea of making binding promises with their servants, God not only gave His word, but by symbolically passing through the pieces of slaughtered animals He staked His very life on it—and we know, of course, that He did ultimately give His life on Calvary to make His promise a reality! Abram wanted more "proof," and did he get it! By passing through the pieces of slaughtered animals, God basically said to Abram, "This is not the body of a heifer or of a female goat; it is My body if I should ever fail to be faithful to the promises I have made to Abram and his descendants." God could have given no greater evidence of the certainty of His word.

Abraham, Sarah, and Hagar (Gen. 16; 21:1-21)

In Galatians 4:21-31 Paul not only speaks negatively about the experience of the children of Israel at Mount Sinai—he also has a rather disparaging view of Hagar, Abram's second wife. Why would the apostle speak about Hagar in such an unflattering manner?

His statements are not so much about her as a person as they are about the role she played in relation to Abram's failure to believe God's covenantal promise. Hagar was not always Abram's concubine-wife. She appeared in the Genesis story first as an Egyptian slave in Abram's household (Gen. 16:3). Likely she came into his possession as one of the many gifts Pharaoh gave to him in exchange for Sarai—an event associated with Abram's first act of unbelief in God's promise (Gen. 12:11-16).

Even after waiting 10 years for the promised child to be born, Abram and Sarai remained childless. In spite of the formal covenant God made with Abram in Genesis 15, he and Sarai concluded that the Lord needed their help. Sarai gave Hagar to Abram as a concubine-wife (Gen. 16:3; 25:6). As a slave, Hagar would not have had a choice in the matter. She simply had to do as told. Although strange to us today, Sarai's plan was quite ingenious. According to ancient customs, a female slave could legally serve as a surrogate mother for her barren mistress. Thus Sarai could count any child born from her husband and Hagar as her own. While the plan did produce a child, it caused all kinds of headaches and problems, the biggest problem being that the planned child was not the promised child.

For some 13 years Abram believed that Ishmael was the son through whom the Lord would fulfill His promises. Finally, when Abram was 99, God appeared to him and told him that Ishmael was not the promised child. The patriarch pleaded with God to accept Ishmael as his heir, but God refused (Gen. 17:18, 19). Why did the Lord decline to accept Ishmael as Abram's heir?

It was not that something was "wrong" with Ishmael. He was a child loved by God just like any child in this world. If something had been wrong with Ishmael, God certainly would not have blessed him (verse 20). The problem was rather with Abram's lack of faith. The birth of Ishmael had come about by the devious planning of Abram and Sarai. They had concluded that if God was going to fulfill His promise, He needed their help. They would have agreed whole-heartedly with the saying, "We do our best and God does the rest," or "God helps those who help themselves." But that was just the opposite of what His covenantal promise was all about. The Lord was not waiting on Abram to "do" anything. God's promise to Abram was all about Him doing something for the human race that they could not do for themselves! The divine plan to bless the entire world would begin with the miraculous birth of a child to Abram and his barren wife Sarai. The only "miraculous" element in the birth of Ishmael was Sarah's willingness to share her husband with another woman.

E. J. Waggoner, an early Seventh-day Adventist author whose perspective on the covenants was perhaps his greatest contribution to Adventist theology,[6] aptly summarizes the foolishness behind the plan for Abraham to become involved with Hagar. "How short-sighted the whole thing was. God had made the promise; therefore He alone could fulfill it. If a man makes a promise, the thing promised may be performed by another, but in that case the one who made the promise fails to carry out his word. So even though that which the Lord had promised could have been gained by the device which was adopted, the result would have been to shut the Lord out from fulfilling His word. They were therefore working against God. . . . It is easy enough for us all to see this in the case before us; yet how often, in our own experience, instead of waiting for the Lord to do what He has promised, we become tired of waiting, and try to do it for Him, and thus make failures."[7]

Hagar and Mount Sinai (Gal. 4:21-31)

Now that we have examined the role of covenant in the Old Testament, and in particular the nature of the covenant God made with Abraham and the role that Hagar and Ishmael played in that story, we can turn our attention to Paul's association of Hagar and Mount Sinai with the old covenant.

When God led the children of Israel out of slavery, as He had promised to Abraham centuries earlier (Gen. 15:13, 14), He desired to share the same covenant relationship with them as He had with their ancestor. In fact, the similarities between God's promise to Abraham in Genesis 12:1-3 and His words to Moses in Exodus 19:4-6 are stunning. In both cases the Lord emphasizes what "He" will do for His people. He does not ask the Israelites to promise to "do" anything to "earn" His blessings. In fact, the Hebrew words translated "to obey" (*shama'*) and "to keep" (*shamar*) in Exodus 19:5 literally mean "to hear" and "to treasure." God's words do not imply some sort of works righteousness on the behalf of the Israelites. On the contrary, He wanted Israel to have the same faith that characterized Abraham's response to His promises. The Lord intended the covenant at Sinai to be one of grace through and through.

This of course raises an important question. If the covenant relationship God offered to Israel on Sinai is similar to the one given to Abraham, why then does Paul identify Mount Sinai with the negative experience of Hagar?

As we saw previously in Galatians 3:17, the covenant at Sinai sought to point out the sinfulness of humanity and the remedy of God's abundant grace typified in the sanctuary services. The problem at Mount Sinai was not on God's part, but rather with the faulty promises of the people (Heb. 8:6). Instead of responding to the divine promises as Abraham did, the Israelites reacted with self-confidence. "All that the Lord has spoken we will do" (Ex. 19:8). After living as slaves in Egypt for more than 400 years, they had no true concept of God's majesty, nor the extent of their own sinfulness. Their response was typical of slaves: "Whatever you say, we will do it." It was not that their choice of words simply offended God. In Deuteronomy 5:28 He declared, "They are right in all they have spoken." The problem was the condition of their hearts. Not only did they fail to appreciate what salvation was all about, but they also had a naive confidence in their own efforts and abilities (verse 29). In the same way that Abraham and Sarah tried to help God fulfill His promises, the Israelites sought to turn God's covenant of grace into one of works.

Paul is not claiming in Galatians that the law given at Sinai was evil or abolished. In fact, he actually never explicitly mentions the "law" at Mount Sinai. He only refers to the experience there as it parallels that of Abraham and Hagar. "Abraham's personal old covenant experience with Hagar was nationalized through the experience of Israel subsequent to God's covenant with them at Sinai."[8] What the apostle is concerned with is the legalistic misapprehension of the law by the Galatians. Like the ancient Israelites, their pride led them to pervert God's purpose in giving the law. "Instead of serving to convict them of the absolute impossibility of pleasing God by law-keeping, the law fostered in them a deeply entrenched determination to depend on personal resources in order to please God. Thus the law did not serve the purposes of grace in leading the Judaizers to Christ. Instead, it closed them off from Christ."[9]

Thus it is important to note that the two covenants are matters not of time, but of the condition of the human heart. Or to say it in slightly a different way, the old and new covenants do not describe "sequential *historical* eras, the first spanning the 1500-year period from Sinai to the incarnation, and the second encompassing the generations following. They describe two different *experiences* based on opposite human responses to the timeless everlasting-gospel invitation."[10] Thus they depict two different ways of trying to relate to God that go all the way back to Cain and Abel. The old covenant symbolizes those who mistakenly rely on their own obedience as a means of pleasing God, as did the unbelieving Jews at Sinai. The new covenant, however, represents the experience of those who, like Abraham, rely wholly upon God's grace to do all that He has promised.

The new covenant is the everlasting covenant; the one true gospel—inaugurated in the Garden of Eden after the Fall (Gen. 3:15), promised and experienced by Abraham and his descendants (Gal. 3:8), and prefigured through the laws and rituals given to Israel. Then God's promise became a historical reality as it reached its ultimate expression and fulfillment in Christ.

The following chart depicts how Paul views the two covenants as two different experiences based on opposite human responses to God's wonderful promise of salvation.

New Covenant	Old Covenant
> Sarah	> Hagar
> Isaac	> Ishmael
> Gentile believers	> Judaizers
> promise	> flesh
> faith alone	> works
> free	> slave
	> Mount Sinai

Ishmael and Isaac Today (Gal. 4:28-31)

Paul designed his brief sketch of Israel's history to counter the arguments made by the Judaizers. His opponents had claimed that they were the true descendants of Abraham and that Jerusalem—the center of Jewish Christianity and the law—was their mother. As for the Gentiles, they were illegitimate. If they wanted to become true followers of Christ, they must first become a son of Abraham by submitting to the law of circumcision. But the truth, Paul declares, is just the opposite. The Judaizers are sons of Abraham, but illegitimate ones, like Ishmael. By placing their trust in circumcision, they were relying on "the flesh," as Sarah did with Hagar, and as the Jews tried to do with God's law at Sinai. Gentile believers, however, like Isaac, were the sons of Abraham not by natural descent but by the supernatural. "Like Isaac they were a fulfilment of the promise made to Abraham   ; like Isaac, their birth into freedom was the effect of divine grace; like Isaac, they belong to the column of the covenant of promise."[11]

In Galatians 4:28, 29 Paul applies the experience of Isaac and Ishmael with that of the true followers of Christ in Galatia. "Now you, brothers, like Isaac, are children of promise. But just as at that time he who was born according to the flesh persecuted him who was born according to the Spirit, so also it is now." The persecution of Isaac that Paul has in mind is likely the ceremony in Genesis 21 in which Isaac is being honored and Ishmael appears to make fun of him. While the Hebrew word in verse 9 literally means "to laugh," Sarah's reaction suggests that Ishmael was mocking or ridiculing Isaac. Although Ishmael's behavior might not sound that significant to us today (all siblings argue and fight at times), it revealed the deeper hostilities involved in a situation at which the family birthright was a stake. Many a ruler in antiquity tried to secure his position by eliminating potential rivals, including siblings (cf. Judges 9:1-6). But though Isaac faced opposition, he also enjoyed all the privileges of love, protection, and favor that went along with being his father's heir.

As spiritual descendants of Isaac, we should not be surprised when we suffer hardship and opposition, whether from within or outside of the church. It "is the double lot of 'Isaacs'—the pain of persecution on the one hand and the privilege of inheritance on the other. We are despised and rejected by men; yet we are the children of God. . . . This is the paradox of a Christian's experience."[12]

Living the New Covenant Life Today

Paul's references to the experience of Abraham, Sarah, Hagar, Isaac,

Ishmael, and the children of Israel at Sinai indicate that his discussion of the two covenants is not ultimately about abstract theological ideas. On the contrary, it directly relates to how God summons us to experience life today. It is not as much about what we should "think" as it is about how we should live. Paul calls us to experience for ourselves God's covenant of grace.

What does that life look like? It is one marked by the peace that comes in knowing that God is faithful to His promises. Filled with wholehearted commitment and daily communion with God, it daily experiences and appreciates His forgiveness and grace and knows the empowering presence of His Spirit that enables us not only to live for Him but to love and care for those around us. In the end it is a life that stands in stark contrast to the old covenant experience into which every human being is naturally born—a life that ultimately trusts no one but itself, that does only what it has to do, a life that does not take God's law seriously or appreciate how desperately it needs divine grace and forgiveness. Ultimately the old covenant is a life absorbed in its own well-being. The old covenant experience is a life of slavery. The new covenant experience, however, is a life that knows the freedom that only God can give.

In contrast to the earlier dispensational diagram of the covenants that limits them simply to a historical time period, the following chart better illustrates Paul's description of the two covenants as they relate to both history and personal experience. By God's grace, may we experience for ourselves the new covenant relationship that He has always wanted to share with us.

God's Revelation of Grace Before Calvary

Creation   Abraham   Mount Sinai

God's Ultimate Revelation of Grace in the Resurrected Christ

The Everlasting or New Covenant Experience:
True Gospel—Faith in Christ—A Spirit-led Life

Old Covenant Experience:
False Gospel—Trust in Self—Legalism

---

[1] Philip W. Comfort and Walter A. Elwell, eds., *Tyndale Bible Dictionary* (Wheaton, Ill.: Tyndale House, 2001), p. 323.

[2] Bill T. Arnold and Bryan E. Beyer, eds., *Readings From the Ancient Near East* (Grand Rapids: Baker Academic, 2002), p. 101.

[3] Hans K. LaRondelle, *Our Creator Redeemer: An Introduction to Biblical Covenant Theology* (Berrien Springs, Mich.: Andrews University Press, 2005), p. 4.

[4] *Ibid.*, p. 19.

[5] *Ibid.*, pp. 22, 23.

[6] W. Whidden, *E. J. Waggoner,* p. 267.

[7] E. J. Waggoner, "The Flesh Against the Spirit," *Present Truth*, June 11, 1896; reprinted in *The Everlasting Covenant* (International Tract Society, 1900), pp. 75, 76.

[8] Skip MacCarty, *In Granite or Ingrained* (Berrien Springs, Mich.: Andrews University Press, 2007), p. 97.

[9] O. Palmer Robertson, *The Christ of the Covenants* (Phillipsburg, N. J.: Presbyterian and Reformed Pub. Co., 1980), p. 181.

[10] MacCarty, p. 94. (Italics supplied.)

[11] J. Dunn, *The Epistle to the Galatians,* p. 256.

[12] John Stott, *The Message of Galatians* (Downers Grove, Ill.: InterVarsity Press, 1968), p. 128.

CHAPTER 11

Freedom in Christ

*F*reedom. Probably no single word resonates more in the hearts and minds of people around the world. Moshe Dayan, the Israeli military leader who became a champion of peace in the 1970s, summarized the value and importance of freedom by referring to it as "the oxygen of the soul." His analogy suggests that without freedom we wither and die—but with it we blossom, flourish, and live. I think he certainly is right. The human desire to be free transcends culture, race, and even age. It is something so cherished that people are willing to risk their lives to acquire and preserve it. In fact, not a single month goes by without some country around the world celebrating their national freedom with a holiday.

Yet strangely enough, even in countries where freedom is a legal right, many people find that it is something missing from their daily lives. How can a person be free, but lacking freedom? Although it sounds like a paradox, it is often true. For, freedom is more than just a national declaration. It goes far beyond a person's right to vote, to fight, to own personal property, or even to do what he or she feels like doing. That is far too simplistic, though that is what we initially think of when we talk about freedom. True freedom strikes at the very heart of who we are and what we are called to be. It is not simply the right to do whatever we like or want to do, but the freedom to do the things we know we ought to do. And it is on this latter point that we often find ourselves falling short. Thus although we applaud freedom, we are often confused about what it really involves and how genuinely to experience it for ourselves.

Although many people might find it surprising, the Bible has much to say about freedom. Of all the New Testament writers, the apostle Paul has often been singled out as the "champion of freedom." And rightly so, for not only does he use the word "freedom" more often than any other New Testament author—it is also one of his favorite terms to describe what the gospel is all about. Galatians, more than any one of his other letters, is associated with freedom. Already in Galatians 2:4 we have seen that Paul briefly referred to the importance of protecting the freedom we have in Christ Jesus. But what does he mean when he speaks about Christian freedom? What does it include? How far does that freedom go? Does it have any limits? And does it have any connection to the law?

Paul addresses all these questions in the process of warning the Galatians of two dangers in Galatians 5:1-15 that threaten their freedom in Christ: those of legalism and licentiousness. Both legalism and licentiousness oppose genuine freedom, for they equally keep their adherents in a form of slavery. As we will see, however, the apostle appeals to the Galatians to stand firm in the true freedom that is their rightful possession in Christ.

Christ Has Set Us Free (Gal. 5:1)

Galatians 5:1 has to be one of the most surprising verses in the Bible. At least it was for me when I first discovered it buried in the middle of Galatians. "For freedom Christ has set us free; stand firm therefore, and do not submit again to a yoke of slavery" (Gal. 5:1). As a youth I had received the impression that all religion was really about was limiting my freedom—a list with far more don'ts than dos. Yet in Galatians Paul says that Christ has set us free for freedom. Here freedom defines the gospel from start to finish. It is the reason that He laid down His life at Calvary, and it is to characterize the way we ourselves will live life. In fact, the apostle so wants the Galatians to understand this point that he is even redundant. Christ set us free so that we could experience freedom. Exactly what that freedom entails, Paul will explain shortly. But before we consider that, we first need to notice what else is taking place in this verse.

The apostle not only tells the Galatians that Christ set them free for freedom, but, much like a military leader rallying wavering troops, also charges them not to surrender their freedom. The forcefulness and intensity of his tone causes his words nearly to leap off the page into action. In fact, this seems to be exactly what he intended. While this verse is connected thematically to what precedes and follows, its abruptness and lack of syntactical connections in Greek suggest that Paul wanted it to stand out like a gigantic billboard. Many translations indicate this by setting Galatians 5:1 off as a separate paragraph by itself. Freedom in Christ sums up the apostle's entire argument, and the Galatians were in danger of giving it away. They had become so bewitched over the issue of circumcision that they were on the verge of surrendering their freedom for slavery. Paul's hope was to awaken the Galatians to their nearly fatal mistake.

It is important to note, however, that his command to stand firm in freedom does not appear in isolation. An important statement of fact precedes it: "Christ has set us free." Why should Christians stand firmly in their freedom? Because Christ has *already* set them free. In other words, our freedom is a result of what Christ has already done for us.

The pattern of an indicative statement of fact followed by an imperative exhortation is a typical characteristic of Paul's letters (see 1 Cor. 6:20; 10:13, 14; Col. 2:6; Eph. 4:1). Scholars refer to it as the indicative/imperative of the gospel. For example, Paul makes several indicative statements in Romans 6 about the facts of our condition in Christ. "We know that our old self was crucified with him" (Rom. 6:6). On the basis of this fact, he can then issue the imperative exhortation, "Therefore, do not let sin exercise dominion in your mortal bodies" (verse 12, NRSV). It is his way of essentially saying, "Become what you already are in Christ." The ethical life of the gospel is not to be a burden of things we have to do to prove we are God's children. No, that is completely backward. We are called to live as though we are God's children, because we actually are God's children. It is a consequence of what God has already accomplished for us.

Second, Galatians 5:1 also appears to include yet another metaphor to describe the glorious truth of the gospel. In the same way that we might slowly rotate a masterfully cut diamond in order to marvel at all its beautiful facets, so Paul has allowed us to gaze in awe at the vast richness of Christ's gift of salvation from several different perspectives: sacrificial (offering, Gal. 1:3), legal (justification, Gal. 2:16), commercial (redemption/ransom, Gal. 3:13), and familial (adoption, Gal. 4:5, 6). Now with the expression "for freedom Christ has set us free," he has another metaphor in mind. The wording echoes the formula used in an event known as the sacral manumission of slaves.

Since slaves had no legal rights in Paul's day, a deity could supposedly act in their behalf to purchase their freedom. In return, the slave, though really free, would legally belong to the god. It was a process called sacral manumission. Of course, in actual practice sacral manumission was merely legal fiction. The slave paid the money into the temple treasury for his freedom. Consider, for example, the formula used in one of the nearly 1,000 inscriptions from the temple to Pythian Apollo at Delphi that date from 201 B.C. to A.D. 100: "Apollo the Pythian bought from Sosibus of Amphissa for freedom a female slave, whose name is Nicaea. . . . The purchase, however, Nicaea has committed unto Apollo for freedom."[1]

The "appropriateness of this practice as a soteriological metaphor that could be adopted by Christians is apparent: the slave is powerless, but the deity does what the slave cannot do. After being redeemed, the slave belongs to the god, 'whose service is perfect freedom.'"[2] While a basic similarity certainly exists with Paul's terminology, we do find a fundamental difference. The apostle's metaphor is not a legal fiction. Nor do we provide the purchase price ourselves (cf. 1 Cor. 6:20; 7:23). The price was far too high. We were powerless to save ourselves, but Jesus stepped in and did for us what we could not do for ourselves.

The Nature of Christian Freedom

While Paul has contrasted the difference between freedom and slavery in the analogy of the two covenants and decisively called upon the Galatians not to surrender their freedom in Christ, he now spells out in more detail what we have been set free from (Gal. 5:1-12), and what we have been set free for (verses 13-15).

As we mentioned earlier, the use of the word "freedom" to describe the Christian life is more prominent in Paul's letters than anywhere else in the New Testament. The word "freedom" and its cognates occurs twice as many times in Paul's writings as it does everywhere else in the New Testament. But what does Paul exactly mean by freedom?

First, freedom for Paul is not an abstract concept. It does not refer to political freedom, economic freedom, or to the freedom to live life in any way that we might please. On the contrary, it is a freedom grounded in our relationship to Jesus Christ. While the context suggests that Paul is referring to freedom from the bondage and condemnation of a law-driven Christianity, our freedom includes much more—freedom from sin (Rom. 3:9; Gal. 3:22) and death (1 Cor. 15:51-56) as well as from demonic powers (Gal. 1:4; Col. 2:13-15; Heb. 2:14, 15).

The Dangerous Consequences of Legalism (Gal. 5:2-12)

When I was a young pastor, I once had an elder in one of my congregations who was convinced the church had heard enough sermons about grace. He thought it would be a good idea if I gave the members a good dose of legalism instead. (He actually told me that legalism was not really a bad thing.) It would not hurt anyone. After all, what was so wrong with wanting to keep the law? While his counsel sounded completely logical from his perspective, Paul would firmly disagree on a number of points.

First, following God's law and "legalism" are not necessarily the same. Jesus and Paul both lived a life of obedience, and neither were legalists. Legalism emerges when an individual places more importance on obedience than they do Jesus. That makes a person's behavior the basis of their acceptance with God instead of faith in Christ. Second, legalism and licentiousness are deadly in a church. Trying to balance one with the other is as foolish as trying to use cancer to combat the AIDS virus—they both lead to death. The only remedy for legalism and licentiousness is the proclamation of the genuine gospel, for both are deadly for the life of faith.

The way in which Paul introduces verses 2-12 indicates the importance of what he is about to say. "Look" (ESV), "Listen," (NRSV), "Mark my words!" (NIV). He is not fooling around. Legalism is deadly, and he wants to make sure the Galatians are listening carefully. In fact, he not only calls for their full attention by his forceful use of the word "look," but even evokes his full apostolic authority: "I, Paul, say to you." If the Gentiles are going to submit to circumcision to be saved (the Greek indicates they had not accepted the knife just yet), and if they want to embrace a legalistic understanding of Christianity, then he wants them to realize the dangerous consequences involved in their decision.

So why is legalism so deadly? Paul mentions several reasons.

The primary problem of trying to earn God's favor by submitting to circumcision is how it affects our relationship with Christ. This is such a significant point for Paul that he basically repeats it twice, first in verse 2 and in a slightly different way in verse 4. Legalism makes Christ's sacrifice of no practical value. At its heart legalism involves a rejection of God's way of salvation in Christ. Paul is saying you cannot have it both ways. It is either Christ's merits or your own—the two are diametrically opposed to each other. If lawkeeping had been sufficient, then Christ would not have had to give His life as a sacrifice. It is important to note here that when Paul mentions circumcision, he is referring to it from a legalistic perspective. Obviously he was circumcised as a Jew, and he even had Timothy circumcised (see Acts 16:3). So the problem was not circumcision in and of itself (Gal. 5:6; 5:15), but the way it was being enforced upon the Galatians as a requirement for salvation.

Paul makes his point in an even more powerful manner in verse 4. "You are severed from Christ, you who would be justified by the law; you have fallen away from grace." His statement is significant for a number of reasons. First, he makes it clear that relying on human obedience for salvation does not simply result in loss of the benefits or "advantages" derived from Christ's death (verse 2)—it separates a person from Christ Himself. And the imagery of "cutting of" at the beginning of verse 4 and the "falling away" at the end suggest that legalism is ultimately an act of apostasy. Verse 4 also stands out, for it is written as if the Galatians had *already* made their fatal decision to submit to circumcision. The element of conditionality in verse 2 ("if") is entirely missing in the original Greek from verse 4, though most modern versions do not translate it that way. The subtle change on his part was likely his attempt to startle the Galatians more vividly with the dire consequences that legalism would force upon them.[3] It would leave them without Christ.

A second problem with legalism is that it obligates a person to keep the entire law. Paul's statement in verses 2 and 3 include an interesting play on two words that sound similar in Greek but have radically different meanings—the words for benefit (*ophelēsei*) and obligation/debt (*opheiletēs*). Christ, he declares, will not benefit them (*ophelēsei*)—rather, they will be obligated (*opheiletes*) to the law. If a person wants to live according to the law, they cannot just pick the ones they want to follow. It is all or nothing. The apostle's point is simple, but one that we often overlook. Keeping the law does not merely entail circumcision, the Sabbath, or the dietary regulations. It means every single stipulation must faithfully be observed 24/7. No matter how carefully someone observes the sanctity of the Sabbath, it is meaningless if they are unethical in certain aspects of their life. As it says in James 2:10: "For whoever keeps the whole law but fails in one point has become accountable for *all* of it." It is all or nothing, as far as the law is concerned.

Paul's third objection to circumcision is that it hinders spiritual growth. "You were running well. Who hindered you from obeying the truth?" (Gal. 5:7). His analogy here is of a runner whose progress toward the finish line has been deliberately sabotaged. In fact, Greco-Roman military circles employed the word translated as "hindered" (*egkoptō*) to refer "to breaking up a road or destroying a bridge or placing obstacles in the way of an enemy, to halt his advance."[4] How does legalism hinder spiritual growth? It causes us to take our eyes off Jesus. When Jesus is no longer the focus of our Christian experience, we end up looking at ourselves. As a result, we evaluate people around us by whether or not they measure up to *our* standards. It leads either to a false sense of self-righteousness, or guilt-ridden despair. In either case, it engenders a faultfinding mentality and ultimately creates division. The apostle compares the results of legalism to the behavior of a savage pack of wild dogs intent on biting and devouring one another (Gal. 5:15). Instead of expressing love for each other, legalism produces spiritual death by robbing us of the joy of knowing Christ and experiencing His grace on a daily basis in our lives.

Finally, Paul says that legalism removes the offense of the cross. "But if I, brothers, still preach circumcision, why am I still being persecuted? In that case the offense of the cross has been removed" (verse 11). How does it remove the offense of the cross? The message of circumcision implies that you can save yourself—and, as such, it is flattering to human pride. The message of the cross, however, offends human pride, because to accept the cross means that we have to acknowledge that we are dependent completely on Christ.

Contrary to what my church elder believed, legalism has no benefits associated with it. It is deadly, no matter how packaged. In fact, Paul was so outraged at the Judaizers for their insistence on circumcision that he wishes in Galatians 5:12 that the knife would slip and they would castrate themselves! Strong words, but not nearly as deadly as the false teachings of the Judaizers.

Freedom Not Licentiousness (Gal. 5:13)

Galatians 5:13 begins an important turning point in the book of Galatians. Whereas Paul has focused entirely on the theological content of his message up to this point, he now turns to the issue of Christian behavior. How should a person who is not saved by works of law live his or her life? What does freedom look like in the life of a believer?

One of the challenges that faced Paul's ministry was the potential danger of misunderstanding that often accompanied his emphasis on the grace and freedom that believers have in Christ. The apostle gives several indications in his letters that suggest such a reaction was a problem. In Romans 3:8 he says, "And why not do evil that good may come?—as some people slanderously charge us with saying." Where did such an accusation come from? From the belief that his message of faith alone promoted a careless lifestyle (see also Rom. 6:1; 1 Cor. 6:12; 10:23). The problem, of course, was not Paul's gospel but the human tendency for self-indulgence. We find endless evidence for this in the pages of history littered with the stories of people, cities, and nations whose corruption and demise into moral chaos directly resulted from a lack of self-control.

In an attempt to circumvent such misunderstanding of his message of freedom, Paul warns the Galatians not to use their freedom "as an opportunity for the flesh" (Gal. 5:13). The word "opportunity" (Greek *aphormē*) is interesting. It literally means "the starting point or base of operations for an expedition."[5] The Greek word for flesh (*sarx*) "refers to the inclination and tendency in the human person to live an existence completely and totally centered on the self."[6] Thus Paul is saying that we should never use our freedom in Christ as an excuse, or as a starting point, for indulging our self-centered desires. But he does even more than that—he also specifically mentions that freedom in Christ does *not* include the right to disregard God's law (verse 14). On the contrary, true freedom in Christ should lead to a life of obedience (Rom. 1:5; Gal. 5:14). And finally, Paul says that our freedom does not include the right to pass judgment on others (Gal. 5:15).

While he often talks about how freedom in Christ liberates us from enslavement to the things of the present world, Paul does not stress that point here. Instead, he emphasizes that true freedom is a summons to a new type of service—the responsibility to serve others out of love. Instead of living for ourselves, Paul calls us to serve one another through love (verse 13). Freedom then is "the opportunity to love the neighbor without hindrance, the possibility of creating human communities based on mutual self-giving rather than the quest for power and status."[7]

Our familiarity with Christianity and with modern translations of this passage often make it easy to overlook the startling power that Paul's words first conveyed. The Greek words in Galatians 5:13, 14 indicate that the love that motivates such selfless service is not ordinary human love—that would be impossible. Human love is far too conditional. His use of the article ("the") before the word "love" (Greek *agapē*) in verse 13 indicates that he is referring to "the" special divine love that we receive only through the Spirit (Rom. 5:5). But what is even more surprising is the fact that the word translated as "serve" is actually the Greek word meaning "to be enslaved" (*douleuō*). By nature the words "slavery" and "freedom" stand in stark opposition to each other. Yet Paul combines the two together to describe how radically different the Christian life was supposed to be lived. Genuine freedom is found not in self-autonomy but in a mutual enslavement to one another based on God's love. Thus true freedom can never exist when we seek to live merely for ourselves. It is only when we are willing to loose "our freedom" that we will actually find it (Matt. 16:25).

Fulfilling the Whole Law (Gal. 5:13-15)

Many have seen the contrast between Paul's negative comments about doing "the whole law" (Gal. 5:3) and his positive assertions about fulfilling "the whole law" (verse 14) as paradoxical. How can he say both things without contradicting himself? The solution lies in the fact that he intentionally uses each phrase to make an important distinction between two different ways of defining Christian behavior in relation to the law. For example, it is not without significance that when he refers positively to Christian observance of the law he never describes it as "doing the law." He reserves that phrase to refer solely to the misguided behavior of the Judaizers who are trying to earn God's approval by "doing" what the law commands.

This is not to imply that those who have found salvation in Christ do not "do" anything. Nothing could be further from the truth. Paul says they "fulfill" the law. By this he means that true Christian behavior is much more than the outward obedience of "doing" the law—it "fulfills" the law. Paul uses the word "fulfill" because it goes far beyond the concept of just doing. It "implies that the obedience offered *completely satisfies* what is required."[8] This type of obedience was rooted in Jesus (see Matt. 5:17). It was not an abandonment of the law, nor a reduction of the law only to love, but the way through which the true intent and meaning of the whole law could be experienced.

Where, according to Paul, do we find the full meaning of the law? Paul says it is in one word—and that word, which was surely surprising to the legalists in Galatia as it is to legalists from any generation, is "love." The entire law of God when boiled down to one single command is the command to love. To demonstrate his point, Paul quotes Leviticus 19:18: "You shall love your neighbor as yourself."

Although the quotation comes from the book of Leviticus, the authority of Paul's statement is ultimately rooted in Jesus' use of Leviticus 19:18. Jesus, however, was not the only Jewish teacher to refer to the passage as a summary of the whole law. The great Rabbi Hillel, who lived about a generation before Jesus, said, "What is hateful to you, do not do to your neighbor; that is the whole law." Jesus' perspective was radically different, however (Matt. 7:12). It is not only more positive (you have to take the initiative to do something good), but it also demonstrates that law and love are not incompatible. Without love the law is empty and cold, but without law love has no direction.

How Shall We Live?

God's marvelous love for a world of lost sinners stands at the heart of what Christianity is all about. It is a love unlike anything our world has ever known. It is that love that prompted God to lay down His life so that we might be freed from the slavery of our self-seeking ways. Furthermore, it is a love that God longs to reproduce in the hearts and lives of His followers. Not so that we may hoard if for ourselves, but so that we might share it with others (Rom. 5:5; John 13:35).

The churches in Galatia, having nearly forgotten all that, had begun replacing love and freedom with legalism and slavery. And instead of serving each other in love, they had turned on each other like ravenous animals. Unfortunately, the mistake of the Galatians is not unique—it has continued to replicate itself like a virus down through the centuries. In Paul's appeal to the Galatians to experience God's freedom and love anew, let us also hear Christ's appeal to us to experience the same. May our experience of God's love lead us not merely to follow the law, but to fulfill it!

---

[1] In M. Eugene Boring et al., eds., *Hellenistic Commentary to the New Testament* (Nashville: Abingdon Press, 1995), p. 463.

[2] *Ibid.*

[3] D. Guthrie, *Galatians,* p. 129.

[4] *The Seventh-day Adventist Bible Commentary,* vol. 6, p. 978.

[5] Frederick Danker, ed., *A Greek-English Lexicon of the New Testament and Other Early Christian Literature,* 3rd ed. (Chicago: University of Chicago Press, 2000), p. 158.

[6] F. Matera, *Galatians,* p. 196.

[7] Sam K. Williams, *Galatians,* Abingdon New Testament Commentaries (Nashville: Abingdon Press, 1997), p. 145.

[8] Stephen Westerholm, *Perspectives Old and New on Paul* (Grand Rapids: Eerdmans, 2004), p. 436.

CHAPTER 12

Living by the Spirit

Robert Robinson's eighteenth-century hymn "Come, Thou Fount of Every Blessing" is one of the most beloved Christian songs ever written. While its spiritual message has warmed and encouraged the hearts of many who have sung with meaning its melodious words, the beauty of the hymn stands out even more when one becomes acquainted with the interesting string of events associated with it.

Like any family, Robert's parents had high aspirations for their son. His mother's hope was that he would one day become a minister. That possibility seemed to vanish, however, when his father unexpectedly died, leaving the family practically destitute. With barely enough money to survive, the family no longer had the necessary educational funds for Robert to attend school. But worse than the financial challenges was the fact that the death of his father had left Robert angry with God. The young man had no interest in ministry. It was the last thing he wanted to do with his life. So at the age of 14 he became an apprentice with a barber in London. While he began learning a trade in London, at the same time he gave his personal life over to debauchery and drunkenness.

Three years later the young man decided to attend a religious revival meeting at which he thought he might have some fun watching the "deluded" Methodists. Instead the Holy Spirit used the powerful preaching of George Whitefield to change the entire direction of Robert's life. Speaking of that night and of the succeeding three years, Robinson made the following journal entry:

"Born again on the Sabbath day, 24 May, 1752, by the powerful preaching of George Whitefield. Having tasted for three years and seven months the pains of renewal, I found full and free absolution through the precious blood of Jesus Christ (Tuesday, December 10, 1755), to whom be honour and glory for ever. Amen."[1]

His journal entry about the ongoing "pains of renewal" indicates that although he was converted on a single night in 1752, he continued to battle against the sinful tendencies in his life. Reflecting on his personal spiritual experience during that time, Robinson, who was only 22, wrote:
"O to grace how great a debtor
Daily I'm constrained to be!
Let Thy goodness, like a fetter,
Bind my wandering heart to Thee.

Prone to wander, Lord, I feel it,
Prone to leave the God I love;
Here's my heart, O take and seal it,
Seal it for Thy courts above."

Not everyone, however, appreciated what he had to say. Apparently uncomfortable with the words about the Christian heart being prone to wander, some hymnbooks deliberately set out to "correct" the hymn. Some simply left out the stanza about being prone to wander from God,[2] while others, such as the *Triumphant Service Songs* hymnal, altered the words to make them sound more victorious and triumphal:
"Prone to love Thee, Lord, I feel it,
Prone to serve the God I love."[3]

Despite such good intentions, the original words of Robinson's hymn accurately describe the nature of the Christian's struggle and the way to victory. As Christians we possess two natures that are in conflict. Paul refers to them in Galatians 5:17 as the "flesh" and the "Spirit." Robinson experienced this struggle between the desires of the flesh and Spirit in his own life and was transparent enough to include it as part of his hymn. But just because our sinful nature is prone to wander from God does not mean that we have to be enslaved to the desires of the flesh. Everything depends on our willingness to be led by God's Spirit. In Galatians 5:16-26 Paul explains how the Spirit can make a life-changing difference in our lives.

Walking by the Spirit (Gal. 5:16)

Verses 16-26 begins with a tantalizing promise: "Walk by the Spirit, and you will not gratify the desires of the flesh." But what does Paul mean when he says to "walk by the Spirit"? And what are the desires of the flesh that he says we do not have to gratify? What would such terms have meant to Paul's original readers? We will begin by examining the latter first.

The apostle's readers were certainly acquainted with the word "desire" (in Greek it is singular, not plural), and it would certainly not have had positive connotations (e.g., Paul uses the same word negatively in Romans 1:24; 6:12; and 1 Thessalonians 4:5). As Jervis points out in her commentary: "Philosophical and religious thinkers in the ancient world understood that desire was intrinsic to human nature and that it was a trap from which it was necessary to be freed. Desire means one makes one's happiness or peace hostage to achieving what one desires, whether it be money, position, or another person."[4] We can see the problem of desire in the following saying of Socrates, as recorded by Xenophon, the Greek historian from the fifth century B.C.:

"Some are ruled by gluttony, some by sex, some by drink, some by stupid and costly ambitions. These are such harsh rulers of the people they govern that, as long as they see them flourishing and capable of work, they force them to take the fruits of their labours and spend them on their own desires; and when they see that old age has made them incapable of work, they abandon them to wretched senility, and try to enslave others instead."[5]

All the ancient philosophical schools dealt with the problem of desire. People did not see philosophy as a detached intellectual exercise for the erudite. Rather, it was a way of living that sought to secure and preserve genuine happiness amid the challenges of existence. The Stoics, for example, believed that one found happiness through living in harmony with nature and by learning not to desire anything in this world. The Epicureans, on the other hand, taught that the answer to happiness resided in retreating from society and keeping a check on desire by living a modest life among friends. The basic answer to the problem of desire in every ancient philosophical system boiled down to the way that one looked at life. "The moral philosophers presupposed that knowledge is the source of virtue, and they viewed themselves as doctors of the soul whose work it was to dispel ignorance and error."[6] Thus right knowledge and thinking, they believed, would lead to right living.

Paul's fundamental solution to the problem of sinful desire is entirely unlike any ancient philosophical school. The reason is that he sees the problem as something different. The issue for him, as Frank Matera so aptly says, "is the power of sin (Greek *hamartia*) which can only be overcome by the Spirit. For Paul the solution to humanity's plight is not knowledge derived from moral philosophy but transference to the realm of the Spirit."[7] Right thinking is helpful, but it will get us only so far. As long as we are shackled with the chains of sin, we also need someone who can free us from them. The apostle says that in contrast to the philosophical approaches in his day, freedom from the sinful desires that want to rule our lives comes by "walking in the Spirit." What does this entail?

"Walking" is a metaphor drawn from the Old Testament that refers to the way a person should behave. Paul, himself a Jew, often employs the image in his letters to describe the type of conduct that should characterize the Christian life. His use of the metaphor may also be connected to the name first associated with the early church. Before the believers in Jesus began to be called Christians (Acts 11:26), they were known as followers of "the Way" (cf. John 14:6). This name suggests that at a very early date Christianity was not merely seen as a collection of theological beliefs centered on Jesus with no connection as to how one lived life: rather, Christianity was a "way" to be "walked." It was, in many respects, a philosophy of how one should live life to its fullest (of course, it included much more than that).

The Old Testament defines conduct not simply as "walking," but more particularly as "walking in the law." For example, Leviticus 18.4 says, "You shall follow my rules and keep my statutes and *walk* in them. I am the Lord your God" (see also Ex. 16:4; Jer. 44:23). The Jews have a special term they used to refer to the rules and regulations found in both the law and the rabbinic traditions of their ancestors: Halakhah. While translators usually render Halakhah in English as the "Jewish law," it actually is based on the Hebrew word for "to walk" (Hebrew *hālak*) and literally means "the way of going."

Paul's comments about "walking in the Spirit" stand in clear contrast to the concept of "walking in the law." He is proposing that Christians should live life by the Spirit and not by the law. Once again, it is not that Paul is opposed to the law—he says too many positive things about it elsewhere for that to be the case. What he rejects is the legalistic way in which some Christians were misusing the law in Galatia. The genuine obedience that God desires can never be achieved by outward compulsion, only by an inward motivation produced by the Spirit (Gal. 5:18). Since it is the Spirit who set us free (Rom. 8:2) and sustains our freedom in Christ (2 Cor. 3:17), it also is only the Spirit who can enable us to truly fulfill God's law (Rom. 8:3, 4; 15:16).

The Christian's Conflict (Gal. 5:17)

The struggle that Paul describes is not ultimately that of every human being, but refers specifically to the inward tug-of-war that exists in the

Christian. Since humans are born in harmony with the desires of the flesh (Rom. 8:7), it is only when we are born anew by the Spirit (John 3:6) that a real internal conflict begins to emerge (Rom. 7:9-24). It does not mean that non-Christians never experience moral conflict (they certainly do), but even that is ultimately a result of the Spirit. The struggle of the Christian, however, is more intense and also unrelenting, because the believer possesses two natures that wage war with each other: the flesh and the Spirit.

Throughout history Christians have longed for relief from this internal warfare. Some have sought to end the conflict by withdrawing from society, such as the so-called Desert Fathers from the fourth century A.D. who lived in the desert, where they hoped to escape the temptations of the world. Other Christians, such as those associated with the Holiness movement in the nineteenth century, have claimed that some divine act of grace (an experience often called "entire sanctification") can eradicate the sinful nature. Both attempts are misguided, however. While by the Spirit's power we can certainly subdue the desires of the flesh, the conflict wages on in various ways until we receive a new body at the Second Coming (1 Cor. 15:50-55). Fleeing from society certainly does not help, because no matter where we go we take the struggle with us. No matter where we are in our spiritual journey, as long as we await Christ's return we will experience spiritual conflict. The fact that it continues in us is actually good news in a way. It demonstrates that God's Spirit is at work in our lives!

In talking about the nature of the struggle between the flesh and the Spirit in the believer's life, Paul says that it keeps us from doing the things we want to do. At first it might sound rather discouraging, as if we are doomed, with no hope of overcoming sinful desire. That is not what Paul is saying in verse 17, though. If it were, he would be contradicting what he just said about not gratifying the desires of the flesh in the previous verse. How then should we understand the two different statements?

When Paul talks in verse 17 about the inward conflict in Christians preventing them from doing what they want, he is underscoring the full extent of the internal struggle we face. Since we possess two natures, we are literally on both sides of the conflict. The spiritual part of us desires what is spiritual, and detests the flesh. Yet the fleshly part of us longs for the things of the flesh, and opposes what is spiritual. Because the converted mind is too weak to resist the flesh by itself, the only hope we have of subduing the flesh is by making a daily decision (Luke 9:23) to side with the Spirit against ourselves. This is why Paul is so insistent that we choose to walk in the Spirit (Gal. 5:16).

So what about Paul's promise in verse 16: "Walk by the Spirit, and you will not gratify the desires of the flesh"? We need to be careful that we do not misunderstand what he means here. He is not promising some sort of sinless perfectionism, as if we will never make another mistake in our lives. It is helpful to note that the Greek word translated in modern versions as "gratify" (*teleō*) literally means "to fulfill" in the sense of bringing something to completion. The difference between "gratify" and "fulfill" is significant. Paul is saying that if we live our lives in harmony with God's Spirit, the sinful desires that we have (and will continue to have as long as we have a sinful human nature) do not have to come to full fruition. Thus "living life in the Spirit does not prevent one from having fleshly desires, but it does give one the power to avoid acting on these desires and so bringing them to completion. . . . While sin remains in the Christian life, Paul is reassuring his converts that due to the presence of the Spirit within and among them sin need not reign."[8] King sin no longer has to rule in the life of the believer. It may cause havoc in our lives from time to time, but it no longer sits on the throne.

These two parallel concepts in verse 16 and 17 we also find vividly depicted in Romans 7 and 8. Romans 7 illustrates the conflict portrayed in Galatians 5:17 by describing the disastrous consequences of those individuals (whether believer or not) who try by their own willpower to overcome the sinful desire of the flesh (Rom. 7:17-23). Although they know what is right, they find themselves time and time again bowing to the demands of desire. In frustration they cry out, "Wretched man that I am! Who will deliver me from this body of death?" (Rom. 7:24). Paul then gives the answer in chapter 8, which corresponds to Galatians 5:16. God covers our sinful lives with His perfect righteousness (Rom. 8:1), and then works in our lives so that "the righteous requirement of the law might be fulfilled in us, who walk not according to the flesh but according to the Spirit" (verse 4).

The Works of the Flesh (Gal. 5:19-21)

Having already introduced the conflict that exists between the flesh and the Spirit, in Galatians 5:19-26 the apostle elaborates on the nature of that contrast by means of a list of ethical vices and virtues. The practice of compiling a catalog of vices and/or virtues was a well-established literary feature present in both Jewish and Greco-Roman literature. Such lists identified behavior to be avoided and virtues to be emulated.

A rather lengthy example of a vice list in Jewish literature appears in the writings of Philo, the prolific Greek-speaking Jewish author who lived in

Egypt during the time of Christ. In one of his books Philo cites nearly 150 vices that will accompany an individual who becomes a "pleasure-lover." Because of limited space (not to mention the reader's patience), I list here only the first 10 vices that he mentions: "unscrupulous, impudent, cross-tempered, unsociable, intractable, lawless, troublesome, passionate, head-strong, coarse."[9] Jeremiah 7:9; Hosea 4:2; Mark 7:21, 22; 1 Peter 4:3; and Revelation 21:8 contain similar though much shorter lists.

Although Paul was well aware of vice and virtue lists, and even employed them from time to time in his letters (cf. Rom. 1:29-31; 1 Cor. 6:9, 10; 1 Tim. 3:2, 3), we notice a couple significant differences in the way he uses the two lists in Galatians. First, even though he is contrasting the two lists, he does not refer to them in the same manner. He labels the vice list as the works of the flesh, but the virtue list he calls the fruit of the Spirit. The distinction between "works" and "fruit" is significant. For as James Dunn writes: "The flesh *demands*, but the Spirit *produces*. Where the one list breathes an air of anx-ious self-assertiveness and frenetic self-indulgence, the other speaks more of concern for others, serenity, resilience, reliability. The one features human manipulation, the other divine enabling or engracing, reinforcing the point that inner transformation is the source of responsible conduct."[10]

In his commentary on Galatians, Timothy George describes the differ-ence between the two lists in an insightful way that deserves repeating: "The 'works' of the flesh are the products of fallen human beings in their devising, conniving, and manufacturing (in the sense of 'made with one's own hands') efforts at self-actualization. From the Tower of Babel to mod-ern totalitarianism, from Aaron's golden calf to contemporary idols of money, sex, and power . . ."[11] But when Paul shifts to the Spirit, the ter-minology changes "from the language of technology to that of nature—the *fruit* of the Spirit. Those who grow apples, oranges, and peaches know that however much they may seek to protect their orchards from bad weather or deadly insects, at the end of the day the produce yielded by a fruit tree is a gift, not the result of human ingenuity or agricultural prowess. Just so, that which the Holy Spirit effects in the lives of believers . . ."[12]

The second intriguing difference between the apostle's two lists is that his vice list is deliberately labeled as plural in number—he refers to it as the "works of the flesh." The fruit of the Spirit, however, is singular. This dif-ference may suggest that all a life lived in the flesh can promote is division, disruption, divisiveness, and disunity—sin has no united purpose, it only fragments. In contrast, the life lived in the realm of the Spirit produces one fruit of the Spirit that manifests itself in nine qualities that foster unity.

Finally, a careful examination of the vices cited by Paul in Galatians and elsewhere in his letters makes it evident that he did not intend his list to be exhaustive—if it had, it would have been similar in length to Philo's vice list. Instead, it appears that he chose representative vices that fall into four basic categories: sex, religion, society, and intemperance. While we could certainly expand the individual vices that he explicitly mentions, his list serves to make a more basic theological point: corrupt views about God lead to distorted ideas about sexual behavior and religion, and result in the breakdown of human relationships.

The Fruit of the Spirit (Gal. 5:22-24)

In contrast to the 15 one-word descriptions of the works of the flesh, the fruit of the Spirit comprises only nine elegant virtues. While scholars believe that Paul organized the nine virtues into three clusters of three, there is little agreement on the significance of their order. Some see an implicit reference to the Trinity by the number three; others believe the three triads reflect the ways in which we should relate to God, our neighbor, and finally to our selves; and still others view it as essentially a description of Jesus. While each view has some merit, the most significant point that we must not overlook is the supreme importance the apostle places on love in the Christian life.

The fact that Paul lists love as the first of the nine virtues is not accidental. He has already highlighted the central role of love in the Christian life in Galatians 5:6 and 13, and he also puts it in first place in his virtue lists elsewhere (2 Cor. 6:6; 1 Tim. 4:12; 6:11; and 2 Tim. 2:22). And whereas all the other virtues appear in non-Christian sources, love is distinctly Christian. All this indicates that we should not simply see it as one virtue among many, but as the cardinal Christian virtue that is the key to all others. Love is the supreme gift of the Spirit (1 Cor. 13:13; Rom. 5:5), and it should define the life and attitudes of every Christian (John 13:34, 35).

The Way to Victory (Gal. 5:16-26)

Although an inward conflict between the flesh and the Spirit will always rage in the heart of every believer, defeat, failure, and sin do not have to dominate the Christian life. As we mentioned earlier, sinful desires remain, but they do not have to reign in the life of a believer. But how can this become a reality in our individual lives and not simply theological jargon? Paul presents five key verbs in Galatians 5:16-29 that show the way to experiencing fully the power of the Spirit in our lives.

First, Paul says we need to "walk" in the Spirit (verse 16). The Greek verb is "*peripateō*" and literally means "to walk around" or "to follow." The followers of the famous Greek philosopher Aristotle came to be known as the Peripatetics because they accompanied Aristotle everywhere he went. The fact that the verb is in the present tense implies that Paul is talking not about an occasional walk, but a continuous daily experience. In addition, since it is also a command "to walk" in the Spirit, it reminds us that walking in the Spirit is a choice that we have to make every day. It means that we are to take action, as opposed to "drifting in the Spirit" or "dozing off in the Spirit."

The second verb is "to be led" (Greek *agō*; verse 18). This suggests that we also need to allow the Spirit to be the one to take the lead in where we should go (cf. Rom. 8:14; 1 Cor. 12:2). The Spirit is to be our guide in life. In fact, Jesus promised that the Spirit would do this very thing in our lives (John 16:13). It is not our job to lead, but to follow the Spirit's guidance. But to do that requires that we learn to discern His prompting in our lives and not to ignore it when we do hear it.

The next two verbs are in Galatians 5:25. The first verb is "to live" (Greek *zaō*). By "live" Paul is referring to the miracle of the new-birth experience that must mark the life of every believer (Gal. 4:29; cf. John 3:3, 6). The fact that the verb is in the present tense in Greek indicates that the new-birth experience must be renewed daily. And since we live by the Spirit, the apostle says we also need to "walk" by the Spirit. The word translated as "walk" is different from the one in verse 16. Here the word is "stoicheō," a military term that literally means "to draw up in a line," "to keep in step," or "to conform." The Spirit not only gives us life, but should direct our lives on a daily basis—once more Paul emphasizes an ongoing relationship with the Spirit as he has done through previous verbs.

The final verb he employs is "to crucify" (Greek *stauroō*) in verse 24. Its use is a little shocking. If we are to follow the Spirit, we must make a firm decision to put to death the desires of the flesh (cf. Rom. 8:13). Interestingly enough, the verb "to crucify" is different than the previous four verbs mentioned in connection to the Spirit. This time the verb is in not the present tense but the aorist tense in Greek—a tense that points to a completed action, sometimes associated with an event in the past. Why the shift? Some believe it must point to our conversion experience in the past, while others suggest it refers simply to the "finality of the act rather than to the specific occasion."[13] Both are possible. While Paul is obviously speaking figuratively, we should not miss the basic point his vivid terminology implies: "The fruit of the Spirit is so antithetical to the operations of the flesh that something drastic must be done to them, i.e., they must be crucified."[14] Crucifixion becomes a reality in our lives as we feed our spiritual life and, with the strength of the Spirit, starve the desires of the flesh. And even in this regard, the crucifixion of the flesh is not something we do in our own strength or by our own willpower. We are only allowing the Spirit of God to do in our own life what God already did for us in Christ on Calvary.

The Choice Belongs to Us

The battle between the flesh and Spirit is an ongoing reality that demands our continual vigilance if we want to be faithful to Christ. We cannot rest on our past spiritual laurels, nor can we rely on the spiritual experience of another. Instead, we must have a new experience day by day. If not, then our lives will slowly begin to look like an untended garden. The garden may flourish for a time, but the longer it is left to itself the more entrenched the weeds become, and the flowers and vegetables begin to wither and eventually die. By God's grace may that never be the reality of our spiritual lives. Instead, may we ever be captivated by God's marvelous love and filled with the life giving power of His Spirit. As the little hymn by Richard of Chichester so simply but powerfully declares: "Day by day, Dear Lord, of Thee three things I pray:

To see Thee more clearly, love Thee more dearly,

Follow Thee more nearly, day by day."[15]

---

[1] Erik Routley, *Hymns and Human Life* (New York: Philosophical Library, 1952), p. 150.

[2] *Praise and Worship: A Gospel Hymnal* (Lillenas Publishing Co.), hymn 56.

[3] Homer A. Rodeheaver et al., eds., *Triumphant Service Songs* (Chicago: Rodeheaver Hall-Mark Co., 1934), hymn 94.

[4] L. Ann Jervis, *Galatians,* New International Biblical Commentary (Peabody, Mass.: Hendrickson, 1999), p. 143.

[5] In Xenophon *Conversations of Socrates* 1. 23, translated by Robin Waterfield in *Conversations of Socrates* (New York: Penguin Books, 1990), p. 293.

[6] F. Matera, *Galatians,* pp. 207, 208.

[7] *Ibid.,* p. 208.

[8] B. Witherington, *Grace in Galatians,* pp. 393, 394.

[9] Philo *Sacrifices* 32.

[10] J. Dunn, *The Epistle to the Galatians,* p. 308. (Italics supplied.)

[11] T. George, *Galatians,* p. 390.

[12] *Ibid.* (Italics supplied.)

[13] D. Guthrie, *Galatians,* p. 141.

[14] *Ibid.*

[15] *The Seventh-day Adventist Hymnal* (Hagerstown, Md.: Review and Herald, 1985), hymn 689.

CHAPTER 13

The Body of Christ

A young minister, as the story goes, once asked a wise old minister for some advice about pastoral ministry. What should he expect? What should he beware of? And from all his years of working in the church, what would the older man have wanted to know if he were to start all over again? The experienced minister slowly leaned back in his chair and then paused for a moment, as if he were reflecting on all his years of pastoral ministry, searching for the best bits of advice that might help the young neophyte have a long and successful ministry himself.

Finally he leaned forward and said with all seriousness, "If you want to succeed in ministry, then you need to be aware from the very beginning what is the worst and what is the best part of the church. Did they teach you that in seminary, young man?"

Surprised to find himself being asked a question, the young minister rattled off a number of random facts he had remembered from his classes. "Well, we did talk about the long and often odd hours that make up the life of a pastor. But we also learned how rewarding being a spiritual leader is, and the special opportunity we have to influence people's lives for Christ's sake. Is that what you mean?"

"All those things are true," the older man replied. "But that is not what I'm thinking about. What I have to tell you is much simpler than that, but far more important if you want to be a successful pastor."

Eager not to miss out on any of the valuable information about to be dispensed, the young minister quickly pulled out a pen and paper and prepared to take notes.

The reactions of the young pastor made the older man smile as he remembered how naive he also had been when he was that age. He knew that the advice he was about to give would probably sound confusing at first and rather ordinary. But nevertheless he was convinced that out of all his years of ministry it was the most valuable thing he could pass along.

"Young man," he said, "this may sound like a paradox; but it is true.

"The worst part of the church is not the long hours, nor the never-ending work that needs to be done. No, the *worst* part of the church is the *people*. But, and never forget it, the *best* part of the church is also the *people*."

As surprising as such counsel may sound at first, I think Paul would agree. I have certainly found that to be true in my years of pastoral ministry. The apostle's letters make it clear that the greatest difficulties he faced were not the problems and challenges of traveling across the Mediterranean world, nor were they with the pagans he encountered along the way. No, his greatest hardships came from those who claimed to be the true followers of God (1 Cor. 1:10-15; 2 Cor. 2:1-5; 13:1-3; 1 Tim. 1:20; 2 Tim. 1:15-17). And it was certainly his experience with the Galatians. The very people he had brought to Christ were questioning his apostolic ministry and his gospel message. Instead of showing love to one another, they were devouring each other like wild animals (Gal. 5:15). Paul's churches were certainly not free of problems!

Nevertheless, he never threw in the proverbial towel. He continued to give his life in service to the very people who gave him so many headaches and sleepless nights. Why? Because he knew firsthand the difference the risen Christ could make in a person's life, and the difference that one changed life could make in the world. Paul had experienced the tremendous blessing the church could be when it fulfilled its God-given purpose of being the body of Christ—the visible presence of Christ on earth. The apostle continued to minister and to serve not because of what the church *was*, but because what he knew it *could be*. In Galatians 6:1-10 he sets before the Galatians an inspiring model of what God summons the church to be by His grace. It is a vision that we would be well to catch hold of ourselves.

Restoring the Fallen (Gal. 6:1)

While Paul has lofty expectations for the nature of the Christian life (Gal. 5:16, 21), his counsel to the believers in Galatians 6:1 is also refreshingly realistic. "Brothers, if anyone is caught in any transgression, you who are spiritual should restore him in a spirit of gentleness." Here the apostle implies that humans are not perfect—that they make mistakes. But even more than that, his comment is not about people outside the church but about the *members* within it. No one is above falling into sin. Even the most dedicated Christians are not beyond making bad choices in life. We are all broken by nature. To make sure that anyone reading it might not miss its important point, several Christian scribes added the phrase "of you" after the word "anyone" when they made their copies of Galatians. This scribal change was not an isolated phenomenon either. It occurs in manuscripts written in Greek, Syriac, and even Coptic (a form of the Egyptian language).

Paul not only sees mistakes within the church as a possibility—he regards it as more of a probability. While this is difficult to tell in an English translation, it is clearly indicated by the original Greek syntax (a feature called a third-class condition sentence). Thus his counsel envisions a situation that is likely to happen in the church at some point of time. Rather than their being caught off guard when it does occur, Paul gives the Galatians practical advice on how to deal with such situations when they arise. A similar example appears in the guidelines he gives on marriage in 1 Corinthians 7:10, 11. After stating very clearly that a "wife should not separate from her husband," he concedes, "but if she does . . ." The apostle was well aware that things don't always play out as they should.

So how should Christians respond when a fellow believer falls into some sinful behavior? It all depends on the particular situation. This is apparent in each of the successive steps Jesus outlines in Matthew 18:15-17 for dealing with a fellow believer who has done us some wrong. The same is also true of Paul's own experience with cases of sin within the church (cf. 1 Cor. 5:1-5; 2 Cor. 2:5-8; 1 Tim. 1:20). Thus in order to apply Paul's counsel in Galatians 6:1 correctly to a given situation, it is imperative that we first understand the precise type of circumstances he has in mind. What is the nature of the mishap that Paul is describing? The answer revolves around how we interpret the words "caught" and "transgression" in verse 1.

The Greek word rendered in some translations as "caught" (ESV, NIV), "detected" (NRSV), or "overtaken" (KJV, NKJV) in Galatians 6:1 is *prolambanō*. Scholars divide over how we should understand the word. In the active voice it literally means to "receive" something "beforehand" (1 Cor. 11:21; Mark 14:8). In the passive voice, as it occurs in Galatians, it has more of the idea of being "overtaken" or "surprised" beforehand. Some have understood its use in Galatians as a reference to someone who has been "caught" or "detected" in a sinful act by a fellow believer. James Dunn describes it as a "fellow Christian whose deliberate unacceptable conduct has come to light despite his or her attempts at concealment."[1] We might label this kind of situation as an "I gotcha" moment.

Such an interpretation seems unlikely, however. The passive use of the verb in other cases suggests someone overtaken by surprise. The Jewish historian Josephus uses it to describe a group of Roman soldiers caught off guard in a battle.[2] It is also employed in the Wisdom of Solomon 17:17, an apocryphal book well known to early Christians and Jews, to describe farmers suddenly seized by fear. Understood from this perspective, Paul is not talking about someone involved in a deliberate act of sin, but rather a person who finds himself or herself "overtaken" by a sin (cf. Prov. 5:22) that under the best of circumstances he or she would have chosen to avoid. Thus Paul is not describing a believer "catching" someone in a deliberate act of sin—rather it is sin that does the "catching." It refers to a believer who suddenly finds himself or herself ambushed or "ensnared by the tempter *before* he fully realizes what he is doing."[3]

The likelihood that the wrongdoing Paul discusses in Galatians 6:1 is not an act of open rebellion is also evident from the specific word he uses to describe the nature of the infraction. The Greek word is "*paraptōma*," translated by a variety of terms in English: "transgression" (ESV, NRSV), "sin" (NIV), "trespass" (NKJV), or "fault" (KJV). The Greek word, however, literally means "to fall beside," and it was figuratively used of a person who makes a "false step." The imagery of taking a "false step" or stumbling fits appropriately with the apostle's description of the Christian life as a walking in the Spirit (Gal. 5:16). Although this in no way excuses a person's mistake, it makes clear that Paul is not dealing with a case of defiant sin (1 Cor. 5:1–5). Rather, he is referring to a mistake in our walk with God in which before we realize what we've done, we find ourselves overtaken by some sin.

How should the church respond in such circumstances? Not by punishment, condemnation, or disfellowship, Paul says, but by restoration. The Greek word translated as "restore" (*katartizō*) means "to mend" or "to put in order." The New Testament uses it of "mending" fishnets (Mark 1:19; Matt. 4:21), and Greek literature employs it as a medical term to describe the process of setting a broken bone. In the same way that we would not abandon a fellow believer who fell and broke his or her leg, as members of the body of Christ we should gently care (Gal. 5:23) for our brothers and sisters in Christ who may stumble and fall as we walk together on the path to God's kingdom.

It is also important to note that the Greek word for "restore" in this verse occurs in the present tense, indicating that restoration involves much more than a single act of intervention. Rather, it should be an intentional and ongoing process that seeks to bring healing regardless of the time involved. I like the way Martin Luther described the restoration process: "Run unto him, and reaching out your hand, raise him up again, comfort him with sweet words, and embrace him with motherly arms."[4]

What a beautiful picture Paul paints of the caring and compassionate nature of the church. It is not to be a place where we turn on the wounded, but where the wounded find healing.

While Paul's counsel on restoring a brother or a sister in Christ follows an example of what appears to be unintentional sin, we should not interpret it to mean that forgiveness and restoration are unavailable for deliberate sin. The apostle makes it clear in 1 Corinthians that even cases of flagrant sin can receive forgiveness as long as a person is repentant—that is, in the biblical sense of the term meaning not simply a sorrow for sin, but the decision to turn away from it.

Beware of Temptation

Paul's counsel on dealing with the wayward also includes a strict warning to those involved in the ministry of restoration: "Keep watch on yourself, lest you too be tempted" (Gal. 6:1). The way he words his warning indicates that it was no trivial piece of advice. The word translated "keep watch" (ESV), "considering" (KJV), or "take care" (NRSV) literally means "to look at carefully" or "to pay careful attention to" (cf. Rom. 16:17; Phil. 2:4). So what Paul is saying is "Keep a careful eye on yourself" lest sin also take you by surprise. To highlight his warning, the apostle also switches from the plural "you all" in the first part of verse 1 to the singular "you." This is no general warning that need apply only to "some" within the church—rather, it is a personal warning addressed to each individual member. As Donald Guthrie wisely observes: "Self-examination can only be individual."[5]

What temptation is Paul warning the Galatians to be on guard against? He does not explicitly say. The most obvious conclusion would be that he has in mind the danger of committing the same sin from which they are trying to restore another. While that may be the case, his warning against becoming "conceited" in Galatians 5:26 may suggest that he is specifically warning them from feeling that they are in some way spiritually superior to the person they are restoring. Here is something that we would be wise not to overlook.

One of the greatest dangers to the Christian walk is a false sense of spiritual pride that makes us think that we are somehow immune from committing certain types of sin. The sobering fact is that we all have the same sinful nature—a nature opposed to God (Rom. 8:7). That means that without the restraining power of His Spirit, there is really no sin we would not stoop to commit if we were put in the right circumstances. A recent book by David Cesarani on the life of Adolf Eichmann, the man at the center of the Nazis genocide of the Jews, provides a sobering illustration of this reality.

At his trial in 1961 Eichmann's prosecutors portrayed him as a genocidal monster whose anti-Semitic views compelled him to join the Nazis and to seek the elimination of the Jewish race. Such a demonized view of Eichmann was a common picture of all Nazis at the time. Cesarani concludes, as other Jews also have done, that such a characterization is completely misguided. Eichmann was no monster by nature, or even a psychopath. That would have made his actions easier to deal with because he would have been different from us. No, he was something much more frightening than a monster—he was a human being, someone with the same propensities to evil that dwells in all of us. Drawing on this unsettling reality, Cesarani states that history makes it quite clear that under the right "circumstances normal people can and do commit mass murder or engineer it."[6] Recent history with its constant racism, fanaticism, ethnic cleansing, suicide bombers, and genocidal killings certainly confirms his assessment. Cesarani ends his account with the haunting words, "Eichmann appears more and more like a man of our time. Everyman as *génocidaire*."[7] His book also bears the ominous title: *Becoming Eichmann*.

While we are often loathe to admit it, the same is true of us in a spiritual sense. Without a new-birth experience, the sin that is common to every descendant of Adam would prompt each of us to crucify Christ ourselves if given the opportunity. The devil would fool us into thinking that we are beyond such actions. He would have us demonize Judas, Caiaphas, Pilate, or anyone else as the individuals responsible for Christ's death. But in the end the New Testament makes it clear that it was the same sin that dwells in us by nature that resulted in the crucifixion of Christ. Such an awareness of our true identity outside of Christ can keep us from falling into sin unaware (1 Cor. 10:12). It can also give us greater sympathy for others who have not been so fortunate.

Burden Bearing and the Law of Christ (Gal. 6:2)

In addition to restoring fallen members, the church is to be a place where we "bear one another's burdens" (Gal. 6:2). The Greek word translated as "burden" is *baros*. It literally refers to a heavy weight or load that is difficult to transport over a great distance. In time, however, it became a metaphor for any type of trouble or difficulty, such as that of a long day's work on a hot day (Matt. 20:12) or even a financial difficulty (1 Thess. 2:9; 2 Thess. 3:8). While the immediate context of Paul's injunction to "bear one another's burdens" certainly includes the moral lapses of the fellow believers mentioned in the preceding verse, the concept of burden bearing he has in mind is much broader. His instructions reveal several spiritual insights about the Christian life that we should not overlook.

First, as Timothy George points out: "All Christians have burdens. Our burdens may differ in size and shape and will vary in kind depending on the providential ordering of our lives. For some it is the burden of temptation and the consequences of a moral lapse, as in verse 1 here. For others it may be a physical ailment, or mental disorder, or family crisis, or lack of employment, or demonic oppression, or host of other things; but no Christian is exempt from burdens."[8]

Second, God does not intend for us to shoulder all our burdens alone. The church is a living entity, like the human body. And as Paul explains in his analogy of the church as a body in 1 Corinthians 12:12-26, what happens to one member affects the rest of the body. Church is to be more than just an entertaining or spiritually fulfilling worship service. It is supposed to be a community of believers who interact and care for each other. And the type of care that Paul describes is not a one-way street. God calls upon us to care for others and to allow others to care for us in turn. Unfortunately, we are often far more willing to assist others to carry their burdens than we are in allowing anyone to help us shoulder our own. Paul condemns such an attitude of self-sufficiency in verse 3 as human pride that refuses to admit that we also have needs and weaknesses. Such pride not only robs us of the comfort of others, but also prevents others from fulfilling the ministry that God has summoned them to perform.

Finally, God asks us to bear the burdens of others because it is through our actions that He makes His comfort manifest, a concept again built on the fact that the church is the body of Christ. We see an illustration of this in Paul's words: "But God, who comforts the downcast, comforted us by the coming of Titus" (2 Cor. 7:6). Notice that "God's comfort was not given to Paul through his private prayer and waiting upon the Lord, but through the companionship of a friend and through the good news which he brought. Human friendship, in which we bear one another's burdens, is part of the purpose of God for His people."[9]

But what is even more significant about burden bearing is that Paul connects it with fulfilling the law of Christ. The phrase "the law of Christ"

(Greek *ton nomon tou Christou*) occurs nowhere else in the Bible, though he uses a very similar expression in 1 Corinthians 9:21 (Greek *ennomos Christou*). The uniqueness of this phrase has resulted in a number of different interpretations. Some mistakenly argue that it is evidence that the law of God given at Sinai has been replaced with a different law, the law of Christ. Others claim the word "law" simply means a general "principle" (see Rom. 7:21), as in how we talk about the law of gravity. As a principle it might mean that in bearing the burdens of others we are following the example of Jesus (1 Peter 2:24). While the latter concept has some merit, the context and similar terminology with Galatians 5:14 suggests that "fulfilling the law of Christ" is another reference to fulfilling the Mosaic law through love.

Paul has already shown earlier in his letter that the coming of Christ did not annul the moral law. Instead, the moral law interpreted by love continues to play an important role in the Christian life. It is the epitome of what Jesus taught during His earthly ministry and also practiced throughout His life and even in His death. In bearing the burdens of others, we are not only following in the footsteps of Jesus but also fulfilling the law. Seen from this perspective, the law is not about legalistic rules and regulations that focus our attention primarily on ourselves—but about how we should love and care for other people (Lev. 19:18). Of course, fulfilling the Mosaic law through love also includes a call to live as Jesus did.

To Bear or Not to Bear (Gal. 6:2, 5, 6)

Some people have claimed that Paul completely contradicts himself on the topic of burden bearing. How can he say we should bear each other's burdens in verse 2, and then turn around in verse 5 and declare that we are to carry our own load? Which one is it? Is he contradicting himself?

What at first may seem like an inconsistency between Galatians 6:2 and 6:5 is easily resolved when one realizes that Paul is using two different words to describe two different situations. As we have already seen, the word for "burden" (Greek *baros*) in verse 2 refers to a heavy load that one must haul for a long distance. The word translated as "load" in verse 5 is *phortion*. It refers to something more general that each person must carry, such as a soldier's backpack, or a child in a mother's womb. Whereas one can easily share the former burdens with others, the latter cannot be. While we may receive encouragement and help from others, there are simply some burdens in life that we cannot escape—we have to shoulder them ourselves. No matter how helpful a husband may want to be, a pregnant

141

mother cannot share the responsibility of carrying her own child. Likewise, soldiers are also responsible for carrying their own packs. In the same way, Paul is saying that there are some burdens that no *human* can bear for us: the burden of a guilty conscience, our own sinful inclinations, or the loss of a spouse or a child. Our only hope for enduring these kinds of burdens is found in the comfort and strength offered in Christ (Matt. 11:28-30).

After his advice on burden bearing, Paul makes a comment that seems rather disconnected to everything else that he has just said: "One who is taught the word must share all good things with the one who teaches" (Gal. 6:6). What connection does this have to burden bearing? Or did Paul intend for it to be an independent statement?

While it is hard to know for sure, it appears most likely that he wanted to be careful that his comments about bearing certain of our own burdens not be misunderstood. It had been his practice not to rely upon his churches for any financial support, though he acknowledges that financial remuneration is a right a teacher or preacher is entitled to claim (1 Cor. 9:3-12). Paul seems to be concerned that the Galatians might mistakenly conclude from his comments that they had no responsibility for providing for the financial needs of their spiritual leaders.

That the apostle has this "financial" aspect in mind in verse 6 seems to be implied in the word translated as "the one who teaches" and the verb "to share" (Greek *koinōnein*). The former comes from the Greek word for "to teach" or "to instruct" (*katēchein*). And it always refers to religious instruction in the New Testament (Luke 1:4; Acts 18:25; Rom. 2:18; 1 Cor. 14:19). Additionally, Paul uses the same verb for "to share" in Philippians 4:15 in which he talks about the financial support that the Philippians so generously "shared" with him. His counsel to "share all good things" with their teachers would also have been appropriate for Gentile believers. Unlike Jews who were accustomed to providing for the financial needs of their spiritual leaders with tithes and offerings, the Gentile world had no similar practice.

In the same way that God calls a church to take care of its members, Paul reminds the Galatians, the members of the church are also called to care for its spiritual leaders.

Sowing and Reaping (Gal. 6:7-10)

Paul rounds out his counsel on the responsibilities of the church with a general exhortation about sowing and reaping to the flesh and to the Spirit: "Whatever one sows, that will he also reap. For the one who sows to his own flesh will from the flesh reap corruption, but the one who sows to the Spirit will from the Spirit reap eternal life" (Gal. 6:7, 8).

Paul's metaphor here is not unique. Jesus makes use of it in His parables (Matt. 13:1-11, 18-23), and it also occurs in extrabiblical writings. It is simply a truism of life. What is significant, however, is how Paul employs it to highlight his previous comments about the flesh and the Spirit in Galatians 5. The apostle's metaphor has two types of soil: the flesh and the Spirit. By the choices a person makes in life, he or she sows either in the soil of the flesh or in the soil of the Spirit. Following Paul's analogy, it is the type of soil that one sows in that determines the crop produced. And as Jesus said, "that which is born of the flesh is flesh, and that which is born of the Spirit is spirit" (John 3:6). The flesh can never produce a spiritual crop, and the Spirit can yield only a spiritual harvest. Everything depends on how a person sows.

We see an illustration of the importance of sowing well in a story told about a group of potato farmers. According to the tale, the farmers decided that they were no longer going to plant the larger potatoes as seed but would keep them for food. Instead, they decided to use as seed only the small inferior potatoes. At first all seemed to go well. The large potatoes were wonderful to eat, and they lasted much longer than the small potatoes ever had. But what started off so well ended poorly. After one disappointing harvest after another the farmers realized that the quality of potato sowed determines the quality of potato harvested. The small potatoes produced a crop of potatoes no bigger than marbles.

If the church is to be all that God has called it to be—His visible presence on this planet—then it must invest in spiritual things. A spiritual investment will not only transform life here and now, but it will also lead to life everlasting. On the other hand, if we sow to the flesh, then we will reap only hurt, heartache, and turmoil—and our spiritual lives and churches will shrivel up and ultimately die. We should capitalize on the opportunities we have now to invest in those things that will yield a heavenly harvest.

So, as Paul says in summary, "let us not grow weary of doing good, for in due season we will reap, if we do not give up. So then, as we have opportunity, let us do good to everyone, and especially to those who are of the household of faith" (Gal. 6:9, 10).

---

[1] J. Dunn, *The Epistle to the Galatians,* p. 319.
[2] Josephus *Jewish War* 5. 79.

[3] W. Hendriksen, *Exposition of Galatians,* p. 231, note 170.

[4] Martin Luther, *A Commentary on St. Paul's Epistle to the Galatians* (Cambridge, Eng.: James Clarke & Co., 1953), p. 538.

[5] D. Guthrie, *Galatians,* p. 142.

[6] David Cesarani, *Becoming Eichmann* (Cambridge, Mass.: Da Capo Press, 2006), p. 368.

[7] *Ibid.*

[8] T. George, *Galatians,* p. 413.

[9] J. Stott, *The Message of Galatians,* p. 158.

CHAPTER 14

Glorying in the Cross of Christ

When the Soviets seized control of Poland at the end of World War II, the Communist Party quickly worked to consolidate its power and began implementing a number of sweeping national reforms. Threatened by the power of the Catholic Church, the government sought to weaken its authority through persecution. In 1961 the authorities officially banned all forms of religious symbols from public institutions—factories, hospitals, schools, and governmental buildings. The ban, however, did not get as strictly enforced in schools as it did elsewhere.

When the Solidarity movement began growing in power during the early 1980s, crosses began reappearing on buildings all across the country. Concerned with such defiant actions, the Polish prime minister decided to crack down. He ordered all crosses removed from *all* public institutions, as stated by law. His decree, however, sparked an unanticipated massive wave of protests across the country. Finally under unprecedented public outcry, the government eventually agreed to overlook the crosses, but insisted that the law remain on the books.

Several months later one zealous Communist school principal decided, however, that the law was the law, and that he would enforce it in his school no matter what. One evening he decided to remove the crosses secretly from seven lecture halls, where they had hung since the 1920s. His actions set off a series of escalating events. A group of parents retaliated by breaking into the school and hanging new crosses in the seven lecture halls. The principal had the new crosses removed and threatened to cancel graduation unless the parents and the students agreed to abide by the law. They refused. And with that, something that had seemed like nothing more than a local controversy ended up becoming a nationwide confrontation between the Communist government and the Catholic Church.

In spite of threats by the government, thousands of students organized a massive nonviolent four-day protest. They attended special Masses, wore crosses around their necks, and carried crosses around as part of a public demonstration. After a long and tense standoff, the government and the school allowed the crosses to remain. While the entire event was amazing to follow as it developed, the most moving scene of the entire confrontation was the simple yet profound words a local priest delivered to a crowd of students to encourage them in their protest. He told them, "There is no Poland without a cross."[1]

As we draw to the close of our study of Paul's Epistle to the Galatians, the message of that Polish priest not only conveys the essence of Christianity but also aptly summarizes the final appeal the apostle makes to the Galatians: "There is no gospel without the cross of Christ!"

Paul's Own Hand (Gal. 6:11)

Paul's final appeal to the Galatians begins with a rather strange comment: "See with what large letters I am writing to you with my own hand" (Gal. 6:11). To understand the significance of his statement, we need to remember the usual way he ends his epistles.

While Paul's closing remarks are not always uniform in his letters, a careful examination reveals a basic pattern that he generally followed: (1) greetings to specific individuals, (2) a personal signature, and (3) a closing

	1 Corinthians 16	Colossians 4	Galatians 6
Greetings	"The churches of Asia send you greetings. Aquila and Prisca . . . send you hearty greetings in the Lord" (verse 19).	"Aristarchus my fellow prisoner greets you, and Mark . . . and Jesus who is called Justus" (verse 10).	
Signature	"I, Paul, write this greeting with my own hand" (verse 21).	"I, Paul, write this greeting with my own hand" (verse 18).	"See with what large letters I am writing to you with my own hand" (verse 11).
Benediction	"The grace of the Lord Jesus be with you" (verse 23).	"Grace be with you" (verse 18).	"The grace of our Lord Jesus Christ be with your spirit, brothers" (verse 18).

benediction. From time to time he also included a final appeal of some kind connected to the overall message of the letter. The previous chart contrasts the way that he typically concludes his letters with his ending in Galatians.

When we compare the main features of Paul's letter-closing formula to his final remarks in Galatians, two significant differences appear. First, unlike most of his letters, Galatians contains no final greeting. Now, the absence of a personal greeting by itself is not always an indication that something is amiss (for example, 2 Thessalonians). But what makes the missing greeting in Galatians highly suspect is the fact that he also deliberately left out the traditional word of thanksgiving at the beginning of his letter. The two absent epistolary features of his letters may be a further indication of the strained relationship between him and the Galatians. Paul is polite but formal. In light of such circumstances it is certainly no surprise that he also omits any mention of extending a "holy kiss" (cf. Rom. 16:16; 1 Thess. 5:26).

As we examine the way he concludes his letters it is important to remember that it was the custom in ancient letter writing for an author to rely on the services of a scribe in the composition of a letter. Peter benefited from the services of Silvanus in the writing of 1 Peter (1 Peter 5:12), and Paul appears to have dictated Romans to a scribe named Tertius (Rom. 16:22). Outside the Jewish world we know that even Cicero, the famous Roman senator, relied on scribes to keep up on all his correspondence. When a scribe finished writing, the author would often take the pen himself and write the last sentence or two with his own hand. We find examples of this practice in the change of script that occurs at the end of several ancient papyrus letters discovered in Egypt. Paul explicitly states in several of his letters that it was his custom as well. In 2 Thessalonians 3:17 he goes as far as to say, "This is the sign of genuineness in every letter of mine; it is the way I write." Such a practice not only added a more personal touch to Paul's letters, but also appears to have discouraged forgery (see 2 Thess. 3:17). We may assume that he followed the custom even in the letters in which he does not mention it.

What makes the ending of Galatians unique, then, is that Paul deviates somewhat from his standard practice. When he takes the pen from the scribe, he is still so agitated and concerned with the circumstances in Galatia that he does not simply write out a short note and final benediction—he adds several paragraphs instead. He simply cannot put the pen down until he pleads with the Galatians once more to turn from their foolish ways.

But that is not all. Paul also calls the attention of the Galatians to the size of his letters. While it is impossible to know for sure what he specifically refers to, there are a number of interesting possibilities. Some have surmised that he did not mean the physical dimensions of his letters, but their mis-shaped form. They speculate that perhaps his hands were either so crippled from persecution or gnarled from leatherworking that he could not form his letters with the kind of precision one might expect from a teacher. Others believe his comments provide further evidence of his poor eyesight (cf. Gal. 4:15; 2 Cor. 12:7-9). While both views are certainly possible, it seems far less speculative just to conclude that he was intentionally writing with large letters in order to underscore and reemphasize his point, similar to the way we today indicate an important word or concept by underlining it, putting it in italics, or writing all of it in CAPITAL LETTERS. Paul wanted to get the Galatians' attention—and he would do whatever it took to do it.

Boasting in the Flesh (Gal. 6:12, 13)

Although Paul has previously hinted about the agenda and motivation of the Judaizers (see Gal. 1:7; 4:17; 5:10, 12), his remarks in Galatians 6:12, 13 are the first explicit comments he makes about them. He describes them as wanting "to make a good showing in the flesh." The phrase "a good showing" in Greek means literally to put on "a good face." It appears only here in the New Testament. The Greco-Roman world also used the word for "face" to describe an actor's mask, and it was even employed figuratively to refer to the role played by an actor. This suggests that Paul is saying the Judaizers were like actors seeking the approval of an audience. In a culture based on honor and shame, as the New Testament world was, conformity is essential. And the Judaizers appear to have been seeking to improve their honor rating before their fellow Jews in Galatia and other Jewish Christians back in Jerusalem. Like David who presented the foreskins of 200 Philistines to King Saul in order to become his son-in-law, the Judaizers wanted to boast in the Gentile foreskins they had acquired as an indication of their own spiritual accomplishments (cf. 1 Sam. 18).

Paul says in verse 12 that the reason some were pushing circumcision on the Gentile Christians was so that the Jewish believers could avoid being persecuted for the cross of Christ. Just what he specifically means by this is hard to determine. Although persecution can certainly be understood as a form of physical abuse, it is important to note that it can be just as damaging even in its more "mild" forms of harassment and exclusion. While Christians certainly suffered physical persecution from their enemies, as they did from Paul before his conversion, they also experienced harassment and exclusion from their fellow Jews for their decision to follow Jesus.

Judaism had significant political influence in many areas. As a religion it had the official sanction of Rome, and many Christian believers would have been eager to maintain strong positive relations with local Jews. In fact, for the earliest years of the church, Christians could freely worship because the Romans regarded them as simply a sect of Judaism. By circumcising Gentiles and teaching them to observe the Torah, the Judaizers in Galatia could find a point of common ground with local Jews. Not only would it allow them to maintain friendly contact with the local synagogues, but it could even help to strengthen their ties with the Jewish believers in Jerusalem who had a growing suspicion about the work going on among the Gentiles (Acts 21:20, 21).[2] Whatever the precise circumstance involved, it is clear that the Judaizers in Galatia were not willing to endure persecution for the sake of Christ.

Boasting in the Cross (Gal. 6:14)

Having exposed the dishonorable motives that prompted the Judaizers' insistence on circumcision, Paul presents his gospel message to the Galatians one final time, though only in summary form. For him, the gospel rests on two fundamental tenets: (1) the centrality of the cross (verse 14), and (2) the doctrine of righteousness by faith, which he refers to by a reference to the "new creation" (verse 15).

Boasting is not typically considered a virtue. We tend to frown on people who like to toot their own horn. But surprisingly enough, boasting has both a negative and a positive aspect in Paul's writings. The type of boasting that he opposes is "boasting in the flesh" (see 2 Cor. 11:18). It refers to every aspect of self-praise that causes us to focus our attention on ourselves rather than on God. The apostle specifically condemns boasting in one's obedience to God's law (Rom. 3:27), the flaunting of our own "superior" wisdom (1 Cor. 1:29), the display of arrogant attitudes by Gentile believers toward Jewish believers (Rom. 11:17), and every form of bragging that takes credit for the gifts and abilities that God has given us (1 Cor. 4:7). And in connection with our passage in Galatians, Paul also rejects boasting in proselytism (Gal. 6:13)—something we as Christians often like to do. Although such behavior may have the appearance of spirituality, it often focuses on our accomplishments more than anything else. All such boasting belongs to the realm of the flesh and is therefore evil (Rom. 1:30; 1 Cor. 5:6).[3]

The positive aspect of boasting that Paul emphasizes likely comes from his background in Judaism and particularly his knowledge of the Jewish scriptures. The Old Testament not only permits boasting in the mighty acts of God displayed in salvation history, but encourages it (Ps. 5:11; 32:11; 1 Chron. 29:11). Such boasting is an act of worship, as well as an expression of thankfulness and confidence in God's covenantal faithfulness. It is therefore the responsibility of Christians to boast in the Lord (1 Cor. 1:31; 2 Cor. 10:17; Phil. 3:3).

What did such boasting look like in Paul's personal life? He boasts in the way that God has worked in the lives of his followers (2 Cor. 9:2, 3; Phil. 2:16; 1 Thess. 2:19). And he even boasts in his own weaknesses, for it is in his weakness that he can see God's enabling grace operating in his life (2 Cor. 12:9, 10). But in the end, as a Christian, there is only one thing that Paul can ultimately boast in, and that is the cross. For it is in the event of the cross that God worked to make all His promises to Abraham a historical reality (Gal. 6:14).

It is difficult for us living in the twenty-first century to comprehend the shocking nature that Paul's comments about boasting in the cross originally conveyed. Today the cross of Christ is a common and a cherished symbol that evokes positive feelings with most people. We sing about the cross, preach about the cross, paint pictures of it, and incorporate it as a symbol on all kinds of religious objects—and many even wear it as jewelry. In the apostle's day, however, the cross was not something to boast in. It was rather something to despise. Jews found the idea of a crucified Messiah offensive. Romans regarded crucifixion as so repulsive that it was not to be even mentioned as a form of punishment suitable for a Roman citizen.

We can clearly see the manner with which the ancient world looked upon the cross in the earliest known drawing of the crucifixion of Jesus. Dating back to the early second century, a piece of ancient graffiti discovered in Rome depicts the crucifixion of a man—or to be more precise, at least the body of a man. Where one would expect a human head, there is instead the head of a donkey. Then below the cross and adjacent to a drawing of a man with his hands raised in worship, an inscription reads, "Alexander worships his god." The point is clear—the cross of Christ is ridiculous. Who would be so foolish as to worship a crucified man? Yet it is in this context that Paul boldly declares that he can boast in nothing other than the cross of Christ!

Every Christian should boast in the cross of Christ, for rightly understood, the cross radically changes how we experience life. It demonstrates God's amazing love and the unfathomable lengths that He was willing to condescend to secure our salvation. Not only does it offer free forgiveness and reminds us that Christ has conquered the grave—it challenges us to reevaluate how we view ourselves, and also how we relate to this world. The world, this present evil age and all that it entails (1 John 2:16), stands in opposition to God. But since we have died with Christ, the world should no longer hold us under its enslaving power. At the cross Christ redeemed us from the present evil age and the powers of darkness. The cross compels us to recognize, as Paul says, not only that we have died to the world, but also that the world counts us as dead.

It was the apostle's vision of the cross portrayed in Galatians 6:14 that captured the heart of Isaac Watts, the famous English hymn writer, and led him to write what some have called "the finest hymn in the English language."[4] His hymn was originally entitled "Crucifixion to the World, by the Cross of Christ."[5] We know it, however, as "When I Survey the Wondrous Cross."

> "When I survey the wondrous cross,
>   On which the Prince of glory died,
>   My richest gain I count but loss,
>   And pour contempt on all my pride.
>   Forbid it, Lord, that I should boast,
>   Save in the death of Christ, my God."[6]

May the cross of Christ inspire and touch our lives in a similar way.

A New Creation (Gal. 6:15)

Having stressed the centrality of the cross of Christ to the Christian life, Paul now emphasizes the second fundamental tenant of his gospel message: righteousness by faith, or as he refers to it here, a "new creation."

Before Paul mentions the new creation, however, he makes a paradoxical comment about circumcision: "For neither circumcision counts for anything, nor uncircumcision, but a new creation" (Gal. 6:15). His statement seems strange at first, since he has been arguing very strongly *against* circumcision. In fact, he has gone as far as to say that if the Galatians submit to circumcision they will be alienated from Christ (Gal. 5:2-4). But now he declares that neither circumcision nor the lack of it really matters. If it is no big deal either way, why then has he written so much about it? What is he really saying?

Paul has spoken so strongly against circumcision that he does not want the Galatians to conclude that being uncircumcised is in some way more pleasing to God than being circumcised. People can be just as legalistic about the things they do not do as about those they actually do. Spiritually speaking, the issue of circumcision by itself is irrelevant. True religion is rooted not in external behavior, but with the condition of the human heart. As Jesus Himself said, a person can look wonderful on the outside but be spiritually rotten on the inside (Matt. 23:27). There has to be something more—and that something Paul refers to as the new creation.

The apostle enjoys using metaphors to explain the wondrous salvation that is ours in Christ. Each metaphor highlights a different aspect of all that Jesus did and wants to do for us. Now at the end of his letter Paul introduces one final metaphor—that of a new creation. The Greek word translated as "creation" is *ktisis*. It can refer either to an individual "creature" (Heb. 4:13) or to all of the "created" order itself (Rom. 8:22). In either case, both imply the action of a creator. And that is Paul's point. Salvation is not something that can be brought about by any human endeavor—whether through circumcision or anything else. He refers to it as "new" because it is something that we do not naturally possess. And it is not something that we merely add to what we already are, a minor adjustment to how we think or even act. Rather, it involves a total change. Jesus referred to this same process in His conversation with Nicodemus, but He called it the "new birth" (John 3:3-8). It is a new birth or a new creation because it is a divine act in which God takes a person who is spiritually dead and breathes spiritual life into him or her.

Paul describes the new-creation experience in greater detail in 2 Corinthians 5:17: "If anyone is in Christ, he is a new creation. The old has passed away; behold, the new has come." Here Paul explains that the act of becoming a new creation includes far more than just a change in our status in the books of heaven—it brings about a transformation in our lives today. Murray Harris compares Paul's expression "Behold, the new has come" to an "Under New Management" sign often posted in large letters on the front of a business to gain attention and announce a new direction.[7] Likewise, when we are united with Christ, our lives take a new direction because we are "under new management." Paul expands on what this looks like in reality in his other letters. For example, husbands and wives are to view and treat each other as Christ would (Eph. 5:22-33; Col 3:18, 19). Relationships between parents and children are to be filled with the love, patience, and honor that only Christ can provide (Eph. 6:1-4; Col. 3:20, 21). And by application we could expand this list to include every type of relationship that we participate in today—all are to be filled with the grace and compassion that we ourselves have experienced in Christ.

All this is possible because it is the result of the wholesale change involved in the new-creation or new-birth process. The new creation involves, as Timothy George says so well, "the whole process of conversion: the regenerating work of the Holy Spirit leading to repentance and faith, the daily process of mortification and vivification, continual growth in holiness leading to eventual conformity to the image of Christ. The new creation implies a new nature with a new system of desires, affections, and habits, all wrought through the supernatural ministry of the Holy Spirit in the life of the believer."[8] From start to finish, the new creation is God's work. It is not something that He offers only to a select few, but rather what He seeks to do in all of our lives—if we will let Him.

Final Remarks (Gal. 6:16, 17)

Before Paul closes his letter with a final benediction, he makes two separate remarks in Galatians 6:16, 17 that deserve our brief attention.

First he states, "And as for all who walk by this rule, peace and mercy be upon them, and upon the Israel of God." Here the word translated "rule" (Greek *kanōn*) literally refers to a straight rod or bar used by masons or carpenters for measuring. The word eventually came figuratively to represent the "rules" or "standards" by which a person evaluates something. For example, when people talk about the New Testament canon they have in mind the 27 books in the New Testament that we see as authoritative for determining both the belief and practice of the church. Therefore if a teaching does not "measure up" with what is found in these books, it is not accepted. Thus Paul is saying that the believers in Galatia are to live life in harmony with the principle he has just laid down in the previous two verses—the centrality of the cross.[9]

Who is the "Israel of God" in Galatians 6:16? Some have understood it as the Jews who make up the nation of Israel as a whole. Others claim that it refers to Christians, whether Jew or Gentile, who are the true "spiritual" Israel. Since Paul does not use the expression elsewhere in his writings, we can appeal to no other verse to answer our question. We may find some help, however, in his Greek syntax. Several scholars argue that "'all who walk by this rule' and 'the Israel of God' are not two groups, but one. The connecting particle *kai* [in Greek] should be translated 'even,' not 'and,' or be omitted (as in RSV). The Christian church enjoys a direct continuity with God's people in the Old Testament. Those who are in Christ today are 'the true circumcision' (Phil. 3:3), 'Abraham's offspring' (Gal. 3:29), and 'the Israel of God.'"[10] Such an interpretation would certainly agree with Paul's earlier claim in Galatians 3 that the Gentiles are also Abraham's spiritual descendants through Christ.

The second statement Paul makes appears in verse 17: "From now on let no one cause me trouble, for I bear on my body the marks of Jesus." What are the "marks of Jesus" that he has on his body? And why should no one trouble him because of them?

The word translated "mark" comes from the Greek word *stigmata*, from which we derive the English word "stigma." Some have seen in Paul's comment a reference to the common practice of the branding of slaves with the insignia of their master as a form of identification, or even to the practice in some mystery religions in which participants branded themselves as a sign of devotion. It is more likely, however, a reference to the scars left upon Paul's body by the persecution and hardship he experienced while proclaiming the gospel (cf. 2 Cor. 11:24-27). Support for this interpretation appears in 2 Corinthians 4:8-10, in which the apostle makes a similar statement about the persecution he endured. After stating how he was "struck down, but not destroyed" (verse 9), Paul describes his experience as "always carrying in the body the death of Jesus, so that the life of Jesus may also be manifested in our bodies" (verse 10)

Rather than a disconnected statement at the end of his letter, F. F. Bruce notes that Paul's reference to the "marks of Jesus" would have had a very appropriate connection to his message and even perhaps his personal experience with the Galatians themselves. In contrast to the mark of circumcision, "Paul asserts that he has marks on his body which do mean something real—the . . . scars which he has acquired as the direct consequence of his service for Jesus. These proclaim whose he is and whom he serves. Among them the most permanent were probably the marks left by his stoning at Lystra (Acts 14:19; cf. 2 Cor. 11:25), and if the church of Lystra was one of those to which this letter was addressed, some at least of his readers would have a vivid recollection of that occasion."[11]

Paul's Final Prayer (Gal. 6:18)

The apostle's last word to the Galatians is the same word that begins and ends all his letters—grace. Grace, it has been said, is the bookends of the gospel. Grace first and grace last—that was his prayer for all his churches. It was the grace that Paul saw poured out on Calvary that had captivated his heart and changed his life. And it is that same vision of grace that he prayed the Galatians would also experience. May we hear, in Paul's prayer, God's desire for us as well.

[1] John Kifner, "Student Protest Swells in Poland," New York *Times*, Mar. 9, 1984.

[2] B. Witherington, *Grace in Galatia,* p. 448.

[3] H. C. Hann, "Boast," in *The New International Dictionary of New Testament Theology* (Grand Rapids: Eerdmans, 1986), vol. 1, p. 228.

[4] Wayne Hooper and Edward E. White, eds., *Companion to the Seventh-day Adventist Hymnal* (Hagerstown, Md.: Review and Herald, 1988), hymn 154.

[5] *Ibid.*

[6] *The Seventh-day Adventist Hymnal,* hymn 154.

[7] Murray J. Harris, *The Second Epistle to the Corinthians* (Grand Rapids: Eerdmans, 2005), p. 434.

[8] T. George, *Galatians, p.* 438.

[9] D. Guthrie, *Galatians,* p. 152.

[10] Stott, *The Message of Galatians*, p. 180.

[11] F. F. Bruce, *The Epistle to the Galatians* (Grand Rapids: Eerdmans, 1982), p. 276.

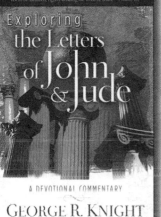
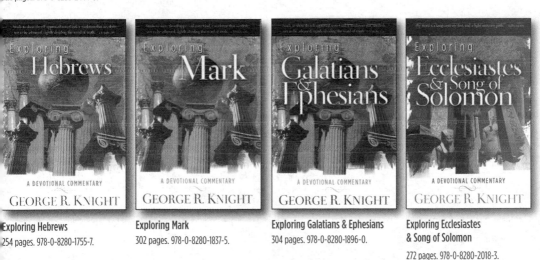

A Bible Study Library at Your Fingertips

The Seventh-day Adventist Bible Commentary Series, CD-ROM, version 2.2
Enrich your study time with one of the finest Bible study software packages available. With just the click of the mouse, you can cross-reference, study in parallel, and search all 12 volumes of the Bible Commentary Reference Series. The commentary links to the NIV and KJV (with in-line Strong's numbers and enhanced lexicon).

Version 2.2a: Bible Commentary. Includes *The Seventh-day Adventist Bible Commentary* (all 12 volumes) plus Lee Gugliotto's *Handbook for Bible Study.* Uses the Libronix Digital Library System's powerful search engine. PC only. 0-8280-1908-8.

Version 2.2b: Bible Commentary Plus Ellen White's Writings. Everything in version 2.2a, plus Ellen White's complete published writings, including books, periodical articles, index, biography, and more. PC only. 0-8280-1909-6.